D0378225

BOB DIAMOND
INVESTOR EDUCATION

How I Make Super Profits in Foreclosure Real Estate Investing

Bob Diamond

1-800-608-0514

www.bobdiamondrealestate.com

Table of Contents

Dedication

This book is dedicated to all those with a dream of financial independence but no clear road map to that goal. May my business systems be your key to the golden future you dream of.

About the Author

Robert L. Diamond is a master real estate investor and real estate attorney. Bob is the foremost expert in showing ordinary people how to make their fortune in real estate. In this book, Bob will give you the foundation and show you how to locate, finance and resell real estate for huge profits.

Bob became involved with investment real estate in 1989. He focused his investing on buying properties he could fix up and immediately resell for a profit in his spare time. In the early 1990's Bob had a deal legally stolen from him by a condominium association due to the knowledge of an attorney working for the association. Then an attorney was given a credit line over Bob simply because he was an attorney, even though Bob had excellent credit and a good track record. This convinced Bob he had to learn more and a legal education would help him to achieve even more success. Bob left the corporate environment and enrolled in Law School. While attending Law School, he worked as a licensed real estate agent which helped broaden his experience.

Bob has learned the real estate business from the inside out. To learn the renovation end of the business, he picked up a hammer and spent three months renovating a house from top to bottom. To learn management, he managed inner city apartments, small rental properties, and single family homes in the suburbs. Bob has bought and sold properties at tax and mortgage foreclosure auctions, from estates, through realtors and directly from owners. He has been involved with over eighty million dollars in real estate transactions.

Bob has spent the better part of two years writing this material which condenses his years of experience in real estate and law into one simple course that gives you the foundations for profitable real estate investing.

A Note to My Readers

I want to wish you the best of luck in applying the material in this book to help you achieve your dreams. Whether it is a home for you and your family or a new business venture, real estate presents incredible opportunities to those who are persistent and knowledgeable.

I have seen many different kinds of people from all walks of life achieve success in real estate. The one characteristic which ties all these successful people together is that they never gave up. When you run into a barrier, don't give up! Work over it, around it or under it!

Success does not come without preparation and work. You take care of the preparation by studying this book, attending seminars, and finding a mentor to teach you. I offer mentoring and coaching programs with coaches personally trained by me. Call my office at 800-608-0514 for more information.

Follow my system and you too can find Your Fortune in Real Estate.

Section One

Getting Started,
the Basics of
Real Estate Investing

1

Introduction to Real Estate Investing

Welcome to the exciting and profitable world of real estate. The goal of this book is to teach you how to find and purchase your first of many properties. I have helped others become very successful and I can also help you.

If you want to make money and save time, this book is for you. You save time because I have packed this book with information which took me years of schooling, investing, and lawyering to learn. You can make a lot of money. Most millionaires in this country are millionaires only because they own real estate.

If you possess common sense, persistence, and a positive attitude, you can be successful. You do not need a college degree, a generous IQ, or a great deal of real estate experience. If you want to make money, this book can help you make thousands of dollars. If you want to live in a neighborhood you never thought you could afford, this book is for you.

Successful investing is not magic, it is the result of never giving up and applying specific learned techniques to situations. Real estate investors can make millions of dollars. I want you to become a real estate millionaire.

Like any business venture, you need specialized knowledge and some money to invest. Right now, you may not have either. Do not worry.

> You can achieve financial independence if you follow my advice and diligently work at the business.

This book will give you the knowledge and experts can be consulted to complement your knowledge in any particular situation. Money can be raised once you find and tie up a great deal. This book will teach you how to gather these resources together so that you can succeed.

Do not quit your job today to start investing full time, but you can achieve financial independence in a relatively short amount of time. If you really want to quit your job then:

- start off part-time;

- diligently apply what you will learn in this book;

- only quit your job once you have the real estate business regularly generating income that can pay your monthly living expenses.

I hope that you enjoy this book, that you will keep in touch, and let me know of your achievements in applying the material.

You can write to me via email at bob@bobdiamondrealestate.com. I also offer live training including real estate investing seminars, coaching, and advanced written courses. Call 800-608-0514 for more information or check out my website at http://www.bobdiamondrealestate.com.

2

Why Real Estate
is a Good Investment

R eal estate investments are the best way for an ordinary man to generate extraordinary wealth without depending on luck, a rich relative,
or the lottery. **Real estate investments have made more ordinary people
wealthy than virtually any other business opportunity or investment.**

There are many reasons that real estate has been an excellent investment in
the past, continues to be an excellent investment today, and will continue to
be an excellent investment into the future.

Investors versus Speculators

An investor is someone who buys real estate he knows is more valuable than
the price he is paying for it or that will provide monthly cash flow net of
expenses. His investment and profit is protected by the value already present
in the property. Investors do the research, calculate the numbers and assure
themselves of the value before they invest their money.

A speculator is someone who buys a property hoping that the value of the property or the rents will go up in the future. **Speculation in property is very risky. Be an investor, not a speculator.**

Benefits and Drawbacks of Investing in Real Estate

Benefit	Drawback
Passive Income	Active investment
Leverage	Not liquid (takes time to sell)
No special qualifications	Responsibility
Monthly income	Lawsuits
Long-term wealth accumulation	
Safety	
Simplicity	
Appreciation	
Tax shelter	
Bargains are available	

Reasons Real Estate is an Excellent Investment

Passive Income: Real estate can provide you with passive income each month. By passive income, I mean money that you make without having to go to work or take any particular action in any month. You can be on vacation and still be making money! Wouldn't that be nice?

Flexibility: The business can be full or part time, and is flexible enough to accommodate most any schedule.

Leverage: Real estate is unique because you can buy the asset by paying for only ten, twenty or thirty percent of its cost. Controlling a large asset with a relatively small amount of money tends to amplify the returns on your investment in real estate and is referred to as leverage.

No Special Qualifications Needed: It is one of the few businesses where an ordinary person without a lot of money, a professional license, or scholarly degree can enter into the business and begin to make money almost immediately.

Top Five Reasons to Invest in Real Estate

1. **Passive Income-** Make money while on vacation!
2. **Flexibility-** The business accommodates your schedule.
3. **Leverage-** Tenants and lenders pay for your investment.
4. **Simplicity-** Common sense business anyone can learn.
5. **Money-** Monthly rent income & long term wealth accumulation.

Monthly Income and Long Term Wealth Accumulation: Real estate can generate regular monthly rental income, as well as substantial profits when the real estate is sold.

Leverage Example:

If you bought a $100,000 investment property with a 20% down payment, you would control a $100,000 asset for $20,000. You are LEVERAGED because you control an asset worth over five times your cash outlay. If your property appreciates at 5% per year, you are getting 5% appreciation on $100,000, which means an increase in value of $5,000 per year. Since you only have $20,000 invested in the property, a $5,000 return is a 25% return on your cash invested!

Safety: Real estate is also generally a safe investment. Real estate rarely sees dramatic or speedy decreases in value. It is also not movable and therefore cannot be stolen from you very easily.

Simplicity: It is a business that an ordinary person with the right guidance, common sense, and persistence can master. You just need some knowledge, guidance, and to go out and apply it.

Appreciation: Over time, real estate generally increases in value. This is referred to as appreciation. If you will think back to what houses in your area were worth twenty years ago, I bet it is significantly less than they are worth today. The people who bought for $50,000 twenty years ago may be able to sell their house for $400,000 or more today. Even if your property does not appreciate by a large percentage amount each year, property values will generally keep pace with inflation. If inflation is as low as it is today, perhaps 2-3% per year, property values will most likely increase by at least 2-3% per year.

Tax Shelter: Real estate is one of the last tax shelters available. With the tax laws, it is actually possible for you to have cash income each month from a rental property and yet still have a tax deduction as though you lost money each month! This is called "depreciation" and is one of the few legal tax shelters left.

The Tax Treatment of Appreciation: You do not have to pay taxes on appreciation until you actually sell the property and realize your profit.

> **'Earned' versus 'Realized' Profit**
>
> You earn your profit when you buy a property at a bargain price. You earn it because you had the knowledge necessary to put the deal together, you worked to track the deal down, raised money necessary to buy it, and had the courage to act when everything was in place.
>
> You realize your profit when you actually sell the property to someone else and receive the money.

In addition, if you die, the heirs to your estate will take the property at the value as of the date of your death without ever having to pay taxes on the appreciation earned while you were alive. The increase in value due to appreciation can allow you to borrow money against the property based on the higher appreciated value. The money that you borrow is usually not taxable, yet you can use it for vacations, an automobile, or virtually anything else that you want.

Bargains are Available: The real estate market is an imperfect market. This means that buyers and sellers do not work with full knowledge of all properties that are available. Depending upon the method used to market a property, the same property could bring a significantly different price to the seller.

If a property is sold through a real estate agent using standard marketing techniques, it should bring full retail value. If real estate is sold at a forced sale such as a sheriff's sale, absolute auction, bankruptcy liquidation, trustee's sale, or other irregular sale method, it is very common for real estate to bring as little as 70-85% of fair market value.

The Disadvantages of Investing in Real Estate

Real estate is not a perfect investment. Here are some of the disadvantages.

Active Investment: Real estate is definitely what is referred to as an active investment. This means that if you have real estate, you must manage it. You must deal with tenants, contractors, bankers, building inspectors, attorneys, buyer, sellers and tenants. You can contract out the management, but your profits will drop. Active investments are in contrast to passive investments which do not require day-to-day management on your part. Examples of passive investments include: stocks; bonds; investment grade diamonds; art work; stamp collections; and the like. I strongly recommend against hiring property managers or buying properties far away from your home unless you have very specific reasons

> **Fair Market Value**
> By Fair Market Value I mean the price a property will sell for if there is no pressure to sell on the seller; no pressure to buy on the buyer; the property is broadly advertised and sold to a retail buyer through a retail method of sale, such as through a real estate broker.

such as an area that is poised to explode. Keep most of your investing and properties local so you can maintain control over your investment.

Real Estate is Not Liquid: By this, I mean that real estate cannot be bought and sold quickly without the quickness of the sale having a large impact on the ultimate sale price of the property. If you put a property on the market, and you want a retail price, you should not expect to make settlement for at least two to three months.

Lawsuits: America is a litigious society. If you are a landlord for long enough, and own enough properties, you will sue other people and you will also be sued yourself. Lawsuits can be simple ones like an eviction, or more complicated ones like defending a lead-based paint claim. The good news is that the vast majority of lawsuits can be taken care of if you buy liability and property insurance on your property. This insurance is usually affordable and covers most of the common things which could happen at your property, such as fire, storm damage, or injury to a person. The bad news is that there are certain risks which insurance companies will not cover under their insurance policies. Those risks include, but are not limited to, floods (most policies), lead-based paint, environmental claims, mold, and fair housing discrimination suits.

Risks not covered by insurance can be minimized with sound business practices and with good asset protection planning. Sound business practices mean that you should take the time to learn the landlord-tenant laws and abide by them. Asset protection planning means you plan your insurance coverage and form of property ownership (corporations, partnerships, etc.) to protect your assets in the event of a mishap. Sound business practices and asset protection planning will greatly reduce your risk of catastrophe. I have a free special report on asset protection planning that you can order through my website www.bobdiamondrealestate.com or by calling 800-608-0514.

If you are going to get into the rental property business, I strongly suggest that you spend a little bit of money, some of your time, and learn how to do landlording properly. If you are interested in learning how to do landlording right, I have an outstanding course which is available through my office. You can get more information by calling 800-608-0514.

People Management: Real estate investing is a people business. You need to be effective in dealing with all kinds of people to succeed. This applies whether you are into flipping properties, meaning buying them, fixing them and immediately reselling them, or renting out properties. These people include tenants, buyers, real estate agents, contractors, attorneys, accountants, and government representatives such as building inspectors.

The most effective way to deal with people as a real estate investor is that you must be persistent, organized, and firm with everyone you deal with. You must be persistent because problems involving real estate often demand action by more than one person to straighten out. You must follow-up, follow-up, follow-up in order to get problems resolved. The real estate investor must be firm because he must insist that others live up to the commitments they make and must not cave in when others try to take advantage. Often tenants do not pay the rent on time, contractors do not perform when they say they are going to, and buyers try to negotiate bargains which you should not agree to. The successful real estate investor must stand his ground.

> ### Should you Incorporate?
> If you are going into business, you should use an entity to do business, I have a free special report on asset protection that is yours for a small shipping and handling charge. See our website at www.bobdiamondrealestate.com or call us at 800-608-0514.

Closing Comments

Real estate is truly a unique investment opportunity for the common man. An ordinary person with some specialized knowledge is able to participate in a relatively simple business which provides:

- incredible tax benefits;
- periodic lump sums of cash;
- wealth accumulation; and
- monthly profits.

> Real estate investing can make YOU wealthy!
> Real estate investments are the best way for an ordinary man to generate extraordinary wealth without depending on luck, a rich relative, or the lottery.

In order to enjoy all of these benefits, the real estate investor must endure small discomforts, annoyances, and inconveniences, all of which are manageable and which do not usually involve large amounts of money, time, or expertise to resolve individually.

3

Motivated Homeowners or Under-Utilized Properties are the Key to Good Investments

There are many sources for you to find real estate to purchase. Sources include real estate agents, estate auctions, foreclosure sales, bankruptcy sales, and property for sale by owner. You need to buy properties with built-in profit. This means buying it for less than full retail price.

You need a "motivated seller" meaning a seller who wants to sell the property. One source of motivated sellers is the foreclosure market. Bargains are often available in the foreclosure market for several reasons. First, the sellers are compelled to sell the property immediately. The property must be sold and settled before the foreclosure date or the property owner will lose the property. Second, the property owner in foreclosure often does not have the money, knowledge, or contacts to sell a property quickly. Third, the property owner typically has financial problems and cannot pay to fix the property up to ready it for sale.

Retail buyers stay away because the foreclosure marketplace appears complicated to the uneducated and time pressures due to a pending foreclosure auction scare away retail buyers. There is often not enough time for a buyer to obtain conventional financing, conduct a home inspection, termite inspection, and other activities which protect the buyer and comfort him. These limitations eliminate most of the retail buyers from the foreclosure marketplace. The people left as buyers in the foreclosure marketplace are professional investors. Smart professional investors do not pay retail price for property.

Another way to make a lot of money is by changing the way a property is used. Different uses of property give the property different retail values. The most valuable use for a piece of real estate is called its "highest and best use." You can make a lot of money by changing the use of a property from one use to its "highest and best use." An example is changing an apartment building to condominiums. I made almost two million dollars on one 12 unit building that I bought for $650,000! I give a course on condominium conversions. You can find out more about the course at www.bobdiamondrealestate.com or by calling us at 800-608-0514.

Save Thousands on Your Next Home!

I think one of the opportunities overlooked by the general public is the opportunity to buy a house to live in for a bargain price at a foreclosure sale. Whatever your budget, there is a foreclosure to suit you.

A house is the largest single purchase and monthly expense most people have. It makes sense to shop for a bargain.

If you do not plan to immediately resell the property for profit, then you can pay more than most professional investors are able to pay. Professional bidders need a 20-30% discount off market price to make a profit. You can win the bids against the pros by bidding just a little more.

Would you like to learn how to buy your next house for 20-30% off? You could save $50,000 on the purchase of a $200,000 property. Pay attention to this book and follow my advice and YOU CAN save thousands when you buy your next house.

I Can Help You Take Advantage
of Many Opportunities...

There are many sources for bargain properties. Sources include IRS sales, bankruptcy trustee sales, absolute auctions, and estate sales.

If you want to expand your capabilities, I teach specialized courses on buying out of bankruptcy and using other specialized techniques to source property.

Check out our website at www.bobdiamondrealestate.com to see our current course offerings.

Section Two

What is a Foreclosure and How Does it Work?

4

The Three Stages of Foreclosure

What is a Foreclosure? Foreclosure is the process by which a creditor forces the sale of someone's real estate to pay a debt owed to the creditor. The creditor can be a mortgage company, the IRS, any local taxing authority, or anyone who has a court ordered judgment against a landowner. Although the exact procedures used to foreclose on real estate will differ from state to state and, to a smaller extent, from county to county within a state, the concepts I will teach work everywhere.

> The concepts in this course work everywhere
>
> Although the exact procedures used to foreclose on real estate will differ from place to place, the concepts you will learn work everywhere.

The Three Stages in the Life of a Foreclosure

Foreclosure can be broken down into three stages. They are: **pre-foreclosure**, **auction**, and **post-foreclosure**, also known as the R.E.O. (**Real Estate Owned** by lender) stage. You can buy a property during any of those stages. We will look at each stage separately because there are major differences in the risks that you take and in the techniques and strategies you will use to acquire property depending upon which stage of the foreclosure process you are buying in.

> **Important Terminology**
> R.E.O. is banking industry lingo for a property a lender has foreclosed upon and now owns. The lender becomes the owner when nobody bids enough for the property at the foreclosure sale. The initials "R.E.O." stand for "Real Estate Owned" and is properly pronounced "ARE EEEE OH."

Stage One: Pre-foreclosure (Prior to Sale)

The pre foreclosure stage is the time period after a property owner defaults on the debt and before the auction of the real estate. During this stage of the proceedings, if you want to purchase the property, you must deal directly with the property owner. The most profitable deals are made during this stage.

Pre-Foreclosure Advantages: There are major advantages to dealing during the pre foreclosure stage.

You have time to:

- work out a deal with the current owner;
- get title insurance;
- have contractors in to look at the property;
- raise money to complete the purchase;
- limit the up-front cash required to buy the property.

In addition:

- you will usually have less competition at the pre foreclosure stage than at any other stage; and

- you also have an opportunity to be very creative. You can often increase your profit by using some of the advanced techniques such as buying liens at a discount.

I have a course on the nuts and bolts of how to buy at all three stages of foreclosure. This is where the most profitable deals are made. If you are interested in that course, call us at 800-608-0514 or visit us on the web at www. bobdiamondrealestate.com.

Stage Two: The Auction (At the Sale)

If the property owner does not stop the foreclosure, the property will be auctioned to pay off the creditor. You and other members of the public will then have an opportunity to bid on the property. The highest bidder wins and becomes the new owner of the property. The foreclosing lenders will bid at the foreclosure sale to ensure that the property sells for enough to pay off the debt they are owed. Traditionally, the amount the foreclosing lender bid at the foreclosure sale was the total debt owed, including late fees, attorney's fees, sheriff's costs and all other expenses incurred by the Lender. This practice assured the lender that the lender would receive either the full amount of the outstanding debt or the property.

After suffering through many R.E.O.s, a few lenders are bidding less than they are owed at the auction to encourage bidders and to avoid being stuck with the property. The lender's attorney will usually tell you the lender's maximum bid if you ask. That maximum bid is called the "upset price. Call a day or two in advance of the auction.

Once you know which lenders are letting properties go for less than the full amount they are owed, keep track of them. You may be able to buy properties at auction which would appear to have too much owed against them to be worthwhile to pursue. This can cut down on your competition and increase your profits.

Advantages of Buying at the Auction: The property can be bought at a bargain price, usually about 70-85% of retail value. The actual price depends upon how competitive your local market is. The process is fairly simple and you do not have to spend time trying to work out a deal with a property owner. This is probably your last chance to buy as cheaply as 70% of retail price.

Disadvantages of Buying at the Auction: Buying at the foreclosure auction has a lot of disadvantages compared to buying before or after the auction. The primary disadvantages of buying at foreclosure sale are:

- high cash requirements;
- disadvantageous terms of sale;
- wasted money and effort preparing for the sale;
- potential title problems;
- hostile former owners; and
- inability to inspect and evaluate the real estate before the foreclosure sale.

High Cash Requirements: You will need a deposit at the sale (usually about 10% of your bid) and to pay in full within a short time (usually one to thirty days). This amount of cash is generally not necessary to buy property at the pre-foreclosure or the R.E.O. stage (after the sale). At those stages, you may have time to obtain financing or perhaps can take over the existing financing. You cannot take out a mortgage on the property you are purchasing at foreclosure sale! This is because banks are not set up to fund properties purchased at foreclosure sales.

Disadvantageous Terms of Sale: The terms of sale at the auction are a big disadvantage. The terms of sale are generally that the property is sold "as is" with no pre-sale inspection. The buyer is not able to have options such as home/property inspections, termite inspections, or mortgage contingencies. The real estate is sold without warranty and without any guarantees. If the former owner is in the property you will have to get him out.

These terms of sale make buying at auction much less attractive than buying at the pre foreclosure, or REO stage. At either of those stages, you can negotiate much more favorable terms for yourself.

Wasted Money and Effort Preparing for the Sale: If you are going to bid on any property at a foreclosure sale, you need to have completed your research before the sale. You need to know the condition of the property, the cost of any necessary repairs, which liens will remain after the foreclosure sale, the retail value of the property, and whether the property owner will fight to stay in the house. This is a disadvantage because you spend time and money researching properties which may not be available by the time the foreclosure sale comes around, or you may be outbid at the sale. Either way, you have wasted time and money.

Potential Title Problems: Problems sometimes arise from the failure of the foreclosing party to notify another lien holder of the foreclosure sale. This will result in the lien holder who was not notified of the sale retaining his lien against the property despite the foreclosure sale. Problems also arise when a second or lower priority mortgage or lien is foreclosing. If a secondary or lower priority lien forecloses, that lien holder retains his lien against the property. If a lien holder retains his lien, you will have to pay him off or risk losing the property if the lien holder forecloses on your new property. Even if he does not foreclose, you will not be able to sell the property until the lender is paid.

Hostile Former Owners: If you buy at a foreclosure auction, the occupants are sometimes hostile. Properties are sold both occupied and vacant. The auctioneer does not generally cause the former owner to move out before or after the foreclosure sale. The buyer must evict the occupants. This can be expensive, time consuming and unpleasant. You should always try to work out a deal with the occupant before you buy a property. I suggest that you do not buy an occupied property unless you have worked out a deal with the occupant or are buying it for no more than 40-60% of retail value, less fix-up costs.

Inability to Inspect and Evaluate the Real Estate Before the Foreclosure Sale: There is usually not an "open house" or any opportunity for the public to inspect property prior to the sale. A property owner may let you in to see the property if you ask. You should always try to see the inside of any property you plan on bidding on before the auction. It is illegal to break into a property without the owner's permission regardless of whether the property is in foreclosure. Get the owner or occupant's permission before you go into the property.

Why Buy at the Foreclosure Sale? The only reason to buy at a foreclosure auction is that it may be your last chance to buy the property CHEAPLY. Properties generally sell at the auction for about 15-30% below retail value. You will usually not be able to buy the property from the successful bidder for such a cheap price after the auction.

Stage Three: The R.E.O. Stage (After the Sale)

Property that has been through the foreclosure auction process and has been sold back to the creditor who forced the foreclosure sale is referred to as an R.E.O. This is a term in the banking industry and stands for "**Real Estate Owned.**"

Benefits of buying at the R.E.O. stage:

- Save 5%-15%, occasionally 20%, on the purchase price of the property.

- Margin is sufficient to find a bargain home to live in or a positive cash flow rental property.
- Spend less time chasing around deals that never come to pass.
- You have time to obtain title insurance.
- You have time to view the property in advance.
- You have time to have inspectors check out the property.
- You have time to obtain financing.
- Properties in very poor condition are often sold at a discount.

Drawbacks of buying at the R.E.O. stage:

- You will pay more for the property.
- It is unusual to get more than 5-10% discount from market, which is not enough of a margin to flip the property.

R.E.O.'s in Strong Seller's Markets

In strong seller's markets (as we have seen from 2001– early 2006) the lenders do not offer very good deals on most R.E.O. properties. The exceptions are properties in very very poor condition because those properties cannot be sold to retail buyers.

I do not spend time chasing R.E.O. properties in strong seller's markets and suggest you do not either. When the market changes consider the R.E.O. strategy.

5

Three Investing Strategies

Now I am going to tell you about three different strategies you can use to make money in real estate. The strategies are to:

- buy the property and immediately resell it ("flipping"); or
- buy and hold for rental.

Strategy One:
Buying & Immediately Selling for Profit ("Flipping")

This strategy involves buying the property at a discount, fixing it up, and then immediately reselling it for a profit. The best thing about flipping is that it gives you freedom from tenant-related headaches. You can make a lot of money flipping properties. Flipping a few properties per year can provide a nice supplemental income generated in your spare time.

While You Are Learning About Flipping, Here Are Some Important Details:

Tax Alert! If you are flipping properties the IRS can classify you as a "dealer." This means that you can never depreciate any rental property you may own. This can cause you to incur a substantial extra income tax bill every year. The issue can be addressed by separating the ownership of property you are holding for rental from those you are flipping. Hold all properties except your personal residence and vacation home in a corporation, trust, LLC or limited partnership, instead of in your own name. Put the properties you are going to flip into one entity and the rental properties in another. The entity that does flip properties can be the "dealer" but that will not affect your other properties being held in a different entity. I have a free special report on tax strategies where I cover this issue in depth you can have for a small shipping and handling charge. Call my office at 800-608-0514 or go to the web at www.bobdiamond-realestate.com to order a copy.

> To minimize cash flow problems, do not get in over your head financially by purchasing expensive properties, or too many properties at once. You should always be in a position where you have enough savings in the bank to pay three to six months' worth of living expenses and investment property related expenses. This will protect you against bad luck, emergencies, or unexpected expenses.

Do the Math Before You Buy: In most situations, you need to buy property that you plan to flip for no more than 70-80% of the retail value, minus fix up costs. You must do the math in advance to establish your maximum purchase price.

This minimum discount may seem high to you. Let me show you why you need such a large margin. The Bidding Sheet Exhibit below shows the profit you should expect to make if you buy a $300,000 house at 70% of retail value. I include a spreadsheet with the course that does the calculations for you. It is called "Flippers" and is very accurate and easy to use. It is included with my investor's essentials forms set. Call my office at 800-608-0514 for information on how to get a copy.

Exhibit 5-1: BIDDING SHEET EXHIBIT
The exhibit below illustrates why you need large margins to be able to "flip" (buy and immediately sell) a property profitably.

Cost	Item
($210,000)	Investors Purchase Price
($18,000)	Real Estate Commissions
($3,000)	Transfer Taxes
($2,500)	Real Estate & School Taxes
($19,500)	Interest (six months of holding)
($1,850)	Title Insurance
($600)	Insurance ($200/month vacant property policy)
($6,300)	Other anticipated costs/contingency reserve
$38,250	Gross Dollars in Profit

Note: This is a simplified version of my famous "flippers" spreadsheet which is included in my forms set. You put the information about your deal at the top of the spreadsheet and then it calculates the profitability. The assumptions which generated the numbers shown above are six months to purchase, fix and sell the property, 13% interest on money you borrow. If you want to purchase my Investor's Essentials form set call my office at 800-608-0514 or visit us on the web at www.bobdiamondrealestate.com.

Strategy Two:
Buying and Holding Properties for Rental

An alternative to flipping is to buy and hold rental properties. The biggest advantage of this strategy is that you will have monthly income in the form of positive cash flow. Positive cash flow means money left over each month after you have paid for the costs of owning the property, including costs such as the mortgage, taxes, insurance, and repairs on the property.

Another benefit of renting your properties is they usually rent quickly. It is unusual for a rental property in good condition to stay vacant for long. It almost always takes much longer to sell a property than to rent one out.

In the long run, you can build up a great deal of wealth with rental properties. If you want to become a full-time investor, you can first build a base of positive cash flow rental properties to provide you with a steady income each month, before moving into the business full time. Then you can pay your bills with the rental properties and make chunks of money by flipping properties from time to time.

How Much Can You Afford to Pay for a Rental Property?

When deciding how much to bid on a property that you plan to purchase for the purpose of rental, the relevant questions are whether you will have a positive cash flow at the end of each month, and whether the value of the property will go up or down over time. Positive cash flow means rent received exceeds the monthly property expenses, including items such as the mortgage, taxes, insurance, utilities, and maintenance.

If you are considering any property as a potential rental, determine your monthly rent, deduct the expenses (mortgage, taxes, insurance, maintenance, management, utilities, vacancy, and repairs) to determine whether you are going to make money each month. Unless you will make at least $200.00 per month positive cash flow per building, $150.00 per month per unit in a multi-unit building, do not purchase the property as a cash flow property.

There is a cash flow valuation spreadsheet included with my Investor's Essentials forms set. This is a precise method of determining the value of a rental property and to tell you if the property will provide cash flow. You can get more information by calling 800-608-0514.

The rules of thumb to decide if you should buy a rental property are:

- Be sure you are going to receive a MINIMUM of $200.00 per month in positive cash flow per building and $150.00 per month per unit in a multi-unit building.

Strategy Three: Purchasing a Home to Live In

You can purchase a home to live in at any of the various stages of foreclosure. You can out-bid the professional bidders because they want to buy at no more than 70-80% of retail. If you bid just a few percent more, you will win the bid. If you are looking for a house priced at $300,000, a bid of 80% of fair market value should win the bid. That would be only $240,000, a savings of $60,000!

Benefits: The benefits are that you can live in a better neighborhood, bigger house and save money! Since a house is usually the largest single purchase families make, saving money in this area will yield big dollar savings to you over your lifetime. In addition, in some circumstances the tax laws allow you to sell your home and take the profit out federal tax free! The basic rule for most people is that you are able to sell a property which served as your primary residence for two of the past five years and are able to take a profit of $250,000 for a single person or $500,000 for a married couple federal tax free! Consult with your tax advisor to check how your taxes would be impacted.

Drawbacks: You will have to be patient and wait until the right house comes along. You will also have to be more flexible about the exact location, house style, and condition of the house you do ultimately buy. There are not nearly as many foreclosures as there are houses for sale through real estate agents. The lower number means you will have less of a selection.

The Property Owner in Foreclosure and Bankruptcy

6

The Psychology of a Property Owner in Foreclosure and Bankruptcy

I have been active in the foreclosure/bankruptcy marketplace for over eighteen years. I have dealt with property owners in cities, suburbs and small towns, black, white, Asian, men and women, young and old. It is amazing to me how consistent property owners in foreclosure and bankruptcy are. They are consistent in their actions, concerns, and how they deal with their problems.

The consistency means that there are some strategies that lead to profitable foreclosure deals, and there are other strategies which are recipes for disaster. This chapter is extremely important, pay close attention and re-read it if necessary.

Paralyzed by Fear:

You will often find that the property owner, especially if he is less educated and less wealthy property owner rather than a more sophisticated or wealthier property owner, is virtually paralyzed by his fear of losing their property to the lender. This fear paralyzes him to the extent that he will not take action to deal with his problem even though that action could potentially avert financial disaster for him. This paralysis is what allows an investor such as yourself to go in and purchase a property at 20-30% less than retail value even if you are purchasing it directly from the owner prior to the foreclosure sale.

Paralysis Leads to Last Minute Deals:

Many pre-foreclosure deals are finalized in the days or weeks prior to the pending foreclosure sale. This happens because the property owner was paralyzed by fear, felt too overwhelmed to act, and instead hoped that by some miracle the foreclosure would be averted without them doing anything. It is not uncommon to find old lottery tickets laying around the house and for people in foreclosure to make a final round of phone calls just weeks before the foreclosure to all of their friends and family to see if they can borrow money to stop the foreclosure sale. Only once the property owner realizes that the game is up, no one is going to lend him money and he will instead lose the property, is he ready to make a deal with you. Expect last minute deals.

Property Owners in Foreclosure are Problem-Oriented, they are not Money-Oriented:

The rational property owner who puts his house up for sale with a real estate agent is typically concerned with getting the highest price for the property. The psychology of the person in foreclosure is markedly different. The person in foreclosure is most concerned with keeping a roof over his head rather than with selling the house for the maximum amount of money. By addressing the primary concern of a place to live, you will successfully deal with persons in foreclosure.

You will find when you first contact the property owner in foreclosure he is embarrassed. You must present yourself as someone who is knowledgeable about the foreclosure process, and who can present them solutions to his problem and solutions to his worries.

Once you show the property owner a solution, it will be as if the property owner sees a door opening into sunlight. He will want to go out into the sunlight of a world with less worries rather than hide in his house, in the dark,

> ### You Are a Problem Solver.
> You should present yourself as a problem-solver for a person in foreclosure. Once you communicate the fact that you are there to solve the person in foreclosure's problem, you are well on your way to gaining his trust and to making a deal which can benefit you financially and the property owner psychologically.

unhappy, worried, and embarrassed.

The primarily problem that the property owner in foreclosure is worried about is that he will be out on the streets and will not have anywhere to live. He is worried because he does not believe that given his credit and lack of money he will be able to get any landlord to rent him a property to live in.

You are going to offer the property owner a solution to that worry and fear.

What you know, that the property owner does not know, is that there are landlords that will accept virtually any tenant if the tenant presents himself properly (neat and clean) and a sufficient security deposit and initial rent is available. Plan on seeing up to twenty properties and putting in several different applications before he is able to find a place to live. I promise you that if the property owner has a monthly income, if they go out to see twenty different rental units that have rent which is no higher than roughly 40% of the tenant's monthly income, the tenant will be able to find a place which he likes and which he can actually rent. Your role is to motivate him to get out there to look at places, even accompany him if you must. In addition, you will enable him by paying his security deposit, first month's rent, as well as assisting him with the money needed to rent a truck to perform the actual move.

You are going to show the property owner that it is possible for him to move from the black cloud of foreclosure he is living with to a place which is clean, neat, and where he does not have a foreclosure hanging over his head. I refer to this as a fresh start. I talk to them about living in a place which is clean, affordable, well- maintained, and where they do not get any surprise expenses like owners of homes get from time to time (roof replacement, central air, etc.). I try to paint a picture in their mind so that they can see themselves living in this new place and can feel in their mind the pressures and burdens that they feel living in a house in foreclosure being lifted from their shoulders.

Property Owners in Foreclosure are Credit Junkies:

Property owners in foreclosure are very afraid of losing their house to fore-closure, they are embarrassed, humiliated and they do not know how to ef-fectively deal with their problem. They are like a dog that knows one trick. They keep performing that trick over and over again even if the trick does not get them the result that they want. The trick the property owner knows is to borrow money and not pay it back. They are often very unrealistic when it comes to their ability to repay money.

When you meet the property owner, one of the first things that they will ask you is if you can lend them the money to bail them out. They are convinced that their luck is just about to change and that all they need is a break. They will tell you a long, sad soap opera story of how they have had bad luck. Do not believe them. There is virtually no such thing as bad luck causing a foreclosure. Foreclosures are caused by poor planning, overspending, and failure to address problems early on. These are not behaviors which lead to success in life. They are behaviors which lead to foreclosure, bankruptcy, and other bad things.

If responsible people are horses and irresponsible people are zebras, then property owners in foreclosure are generally zebras. Zebras do not become horses. You should not expect an irresponsible property owner who has gotten to the point where they are going to lose the roof over their head to suddenly become responsible because you showed up on the scene.

When property owners ask if you can lend them money, you should simply tell them that you are not a lender and that you do not lend money to people, that you are an investor and that you help people solve problems with foreclosure but do not lend money. The property owner's next ploy will typically be asking you how they can stay in the house. They will want to rent the house from you and buy it back at some future time. You should not agree to this. If you do agree to rent the property to the property owner, factor in the cost of an eviction. You will very likely find yourself in court with this person in the not-too-distant future and you will definitely find yourself not being paid as promised. Remember, they are zebras. They do not pay their bills. If you become a creditor, you will be treated like the creditors before you. You will not be paid. You may also find yourself being sued for fraud, unfair trade practices and under other legal theories. In some states such as California, New York, Illinois, Minnesota, and Maryland, you may even find yourself subject to statutory fines, lawsuits and even jail time! Be sure to check with your attorney if there are laws that limit or control your dealings with property owners in foreclosure.

Never Lend Money to Someone in Foreclosure

Most property owners are going to ask you to lend them money to reinstate their mortgage or somehow resolve their problem. People in foreclosure are like drug addicts; they think that their next credit fix will solve their problem. DO NOT BE FOOLED. NEVER LEND MONEY TO SOMEONE IN FORECLOSURE! It is a huge mistake, and you will end up losing your money and possibly being sued. You are not a lender. Do not go where professional lenders fear to tread.

Property Owners in Foreclosure/Bankruptcy Blame Others for Their Mess:

The property owners in foreclosure and who have failed at bankruptcy do not take personal responsibility for the mess they have gotten themselves into. Instead, they blame the lender who is foreclosing, the government, their last employer, the IRS, their ex-spouse, and anyone else who comes to mind. Some of these theories will have some truth to them. In the final analysis, however, the property owner is in foreclosure because they are not keeping a commitment. A commitment they made to pay a mortgage on time each month. They are sitting talking with you a few days or weeks before foreclosure because once they failed to make payments, they failed to deal with their problems promptly, and have instead ignored them until they were on the eve of their house being forcibly sold out from under them. For whatever reason, the property owners cannot accept responsibility for their part in this and instead blame everybody else for their problems. Remember, they typically could have solved their problem by simply selling their house as soon as they had a problem making their payments. They could then rent something affordable for them. The property owner did not do that, so now they are facing a foreclosure sale blaming everyone else for their problems.

Property Owners in Foreclosure Do Not Keep Commitments:

Count on the fact that the property owner in foreclosure will not keep the commitments he makes to you, whether it is something as simple as meeting you at 1:00 at the house, or something more complicated and serious like moving out of the house on a certain date, or repaying you money he has borrowed. The strategy you will use to successfully deal with this irresponsible person, who blames everyone else for his mess, and who will not keep commitments, is that you will not give the property owner any money and will not stop the foreclosure sale until the property owner performs his part.

His part is going to be to go to settlement with you and sign a lease, or move out of the house.

People in Foreclosure Despise Those to Whom They Owe Money:

If you talk to the property owner about the mortgage company or a creditor who is foreclosing, he will typically describe the foreclosing creditor with many colorful words stating how mean, unfair, and cruel the creditor is. When he first borrowed the money the property owner thought these people

> ### Commandments of Foreclosure
> 1. If you become a person the property owner owes money to, he will soon hate and despise you.
>
> 2. Lending money to someone in foreclosure is the express route to lawsuits.
>
> 3. The alternate highway to lawsuits is allowing a former owner to stay in a property.

ple were the nicest people in the world. They lent him eighty percent or more of the money to buy his house. Do you think it is really unreasonable for a lender who lent someone 80% of the money necessary to buy a house to demand that they be given the house back if the person who paid only 20% wants to keep it without paying them? Remember that the property owner hates the people he owes and cannot repay. *If you become a person the property owner owes money to, he will soon hate and despise you as well.*

> ### Important Concept
> The property owner in foreclosure is often overwhelmed by their problems, afraid to act, and irresponsible.
>
> They will often sell you a house cheaply enough for you to make a handsome profit as long as you address their primary problems of finding an affordable place to live.

Summary:

In summary, when you are dealing with a person in foreclosure, you are dealing with someone who is overwhelmed by their problems, afraid to act, and irresponsible. They are often not money-oriented and will gladly sell you a house cheaply enough for you to make a handsome profit as long as you address their primary problems of finding an affordable place to live, assisting them with the money they need to acquire an apartment, and help with the money needed to move their things.

The successful strategy for dealing with the property owner in foreclosure is to help them solve their problem of keeping a roof over their head, finding a new place to live, and handling the moving expenses (security deposit, first and last month's rent, moving expenses). Solve these problems, but be sure to stay in control by gaining ownership of the property and allowing them to stay only if they sign a lease.

The mistakes you should avoid are:

• relieving the pressure of a pending foreclosure prior to getting the deed and short term lease signed;

• lending money; or

• agreeing to rent the property to the former owner for a long time period with any expectation on their part they will be able to repurchase the property; or agreeing to sell it back to them at any future time. In some states, this can subject you to criminal and civil liability.

7

Techniques and Tips for Contacting and Dealing with the Property Owner

It All Starts With Contact With the Property Owner.

All the best deals start with contact with the property owner. Whether it is by an inquiry to your website, post-card, letter, telephone, or in person, contact with the property owner is the key event that makes a great deal possible. The current owner is the only one who can transfer ownership of the property to you.

Information provided by the property owner will help you to understand the challenges presented by a particular deal and put together a workable solution. Even if a deal cannot ultimately be worked out, you will find out about the condition of the property and the attitude of the property owner. These are two key factors to consider in buying any foreclosure at any stage in the foreclosure process. Lets talk now about some methods of contacting the property owner.

Send Letters and Postcards.

If you are pursuing pre-foreclosure and bankruptcy deals you must send out letters and postcards to property owners in foreclosure and failing out of bankruptcy. The letters should state that you can help them to solve their problems. I have included some sample letters for you in this book and on the forms disk. The words that the property owners want to hear are that you will lend them money. If you are willing to lend in some circumstances, you should put that in your letter because it will certainly generate a lot of phone calls. Do not EVER make a false statement in any letter you send or distribute. There are plenty of consumer protection laws you can run afoul of and misrepresentations will get you in legal trouble.

If you are in an urban area with lots of investors a typical response rate for letters you send to homeowners from the pre-foreclosure lists (not the bankruptcy lists) is .75 to 1.5%. Using that response rate, if you send 500 letters you should get

> It does take a lot of letters to find a transaction. The good news is those deals should be worth tens of thousands of dollars to you. The bad news is that you need to send a lot of letters!
>
> I have an automated service that can create and send professional mailings for you. Go to my website bobdiamondrealestate.com for more information.

between three and seven calls. Out of those calls, about fifteen percent of them will be deals for you. The bankruptcy lists are much more productive. Typical response rates are 4% - 8% meaning you get 20 – 40 calls per 500 letters!

Your letters should be short, one page or less, and should state that you can help them stop the foreclosure, relieve their worries and that your service is free.

Some investors also offer adjunct services such as credit repair, negotiation with foreclosing lenders to restructure debt, and referral to refinancing sources. Those services are designed to get the property owner in foreclosure to call, to generate some income, and to establish a relationship with a property owner. The investors using the adjunct services method assume if the restructuring or refinancing does not work out they will be first in the property owner's mind when it comes to selling to an investor. If you are using the adjunct services to establish a relationship then be truthful about what you do. Do not use the adjunct service as a ruse to lure a property owner to dealing with you if your intent is not to perform the service in a competent and professional way.

If the property owner hires you to perform a service, work hard and do all you can for them. If the service does not end up stopping the foreclosure be clear with the property owner why the service failed to permanently stop the foreclosure. If you now want to propose buying the property be sure to explain to the property owner that you want to buy the property as an alternative to the service. Be sure to have the property owner sign the disclosure forms included with the forms set.

If you send letters in a series you should mark the first letter you send "DO NOT FORWARD -- RETURN ADDRESS CORRECTION REQUESTED" on the front. This way, if the person has moved, instead of forwarding the letter the post office may return the letter to you with the person's new address. This will give you several valuable pieces of information. First, you will note that the property owner has moved out of the property, which is a good indicator that the owner is willing to sell the property. Second, you may have the owner's

> The secret to successful mailings is to repeat the mailings. Over 70% of people who respond to direct mail campaigns will do so after the fourth letter they receive. If you are in a state with a short foreclosure (for example Texas with a 21 day foreclosure process) send six letters, one per day to the property owner. If you are in a state with a longer process send letters every ten days.

forwarding address which will make it easy to get in touch with them.

If you are visiting an owner and do not find him home, you should hand deliver a flyer or letter, letting him know that you stopped by and that you would be interested in talking to him. Be sure to put the flyer in a sealed envelope addressed to the property owner so his children or neighbors will not accidentally see it. I have also left post-it notes on people's doors that say "Call me, (215) 555-1212, Bob."

Quick Insider Tip:

If you do the following, your letter is more likely to be opened:

- Put the letter or flyer in an odd size or colored envelope. Do not use business envelopes. I like the Staples brand 5 ½ x 4 ¼ colored invitations style envelopes. They come in packs of pastel blue, yellow and green. An 8 ½ x 11 piece of paper folded in half fits inside;

- If you are hand delivering the envelope be sure to mark "Hand Delivered" on it;

- Address the envelope by hand in blue ink or using a convincing hand-writing font.

Hand Deliver Flyers or Business Cards:

Property owners sometimes will not be there when you stop by. You should be equipped with flyers or business cards to leave at their house. Sample flyers and marketing slogans to base your own flyers upon follow this section. Feel free to use my samples or make up your own and test them out.

Any flyer or letter should be one page or less, and should state that you can help them stop the foreclosure and/or get them out from under bankruptcy relieve their worries and that your service is free. The marketing slogans appearing below can help you formulate marketing materials on a theme.

Keep your flyer design clean. Don't over-crowd the flyer or letter with multiple colors, fonts, and font styles. You want your message to come across loud and clear. Do not let your message get lost in the clutter.

Since these flyers mention foreclosure or bankruptcy, be sure to seal those flyers in an envelope so the neighbors or the children do not see the content of the message. That will only get you an angry homeowner rather than a happy customer!

Here are twenty-one marketing slogans that should resonate with homeowners in foreclosure and/or bankruptcy. You can build marketing campaigns with post-cards, letters and leave-behinds around these slogans:

- No equity, no problem, we can still help.
- Sell your house "as is" for a great price.
- We specialize in creating a solution to real estate problems that others can't touch.
- We buy houses – any area – any condition – all price ranges.
- We help you take control of your situation.
- We are foreclosure problem- solvers and we're here to help you!
- No-nonsense Sheriff's sale solutions.
- Solutions for Problem properties.
- We are the light at the end of your foreclosure tunnel.
- Avoid foreclosure, deal with a professional.
- Foreclosure, learn your options call…. 800-555-1212.
- Quick and easy solutions to your financial dilemma.
- Can't sleep at night, call us.
- I can help you relieve your foreclosure headache.

- Know your options – know your resources, end your foreclosure and bankruptcy nightmare.

- See beyond foreclosure and bankruptcy to a brand new day.

- Foreclosure doesn't have to be a four letter word.

- Instead of walking away, run away today, we buy any houses any condition.

- Freedom from foreclosure.

- You are one call away from peace of mind.

Note: You should test marketing programs against one another. Do not be afraid to run two campaigns against one another to see which one performs better.

Phone Calls:

Phone calls are great if you can get the property owner on the phone. Use the call script on the forms disk to help you ask the right questions. I like to make an appointment to meet with the owner rather than hold a long telephone discussion so I can see the inside of the property. I need to see the property because the condition of the property and the costs to repair it will effect the money and solutions I am willing to offer the property owner.

If you are offering an adjunct service to the property owner be careful not to run afoul of the "do not call" laws. Do not telephone trying to sell your adjunct service. Telephone asking about purchasing the property.

Door-Knocking:

This is the most effective method for finding deals in lower middle class and less wealthy neighborhoods. You will either knock on the door yourself or send someone to knock on the door to talk to the property owner.

The idea of knocking on the door of a property owner in foreclosure or bankruptcy and meeting him in person probably frightens or intimidates you. That is normal. This is a powerful method of marketing and you should add it into your marketing efforts. If you don't want to do it, hire the work out.

You should compensate door knockers for the number of qualified leads they bring in or for the number of deals closed. Do not pay them hourly. It is essentially a commissioned sales job. You want someone who is fearless and motivated. Send them out with the call script and some information about the lead (such as when the foreclosure sale will be held, or when the bankruptcy failed, owner name). Have them fill in the long or short foreclosure information form (see the index of this book for a copy or print it from the forms diskette) and bring it back to you.

Visit When Property Owners are Likely to be Home:

In most cases, the best time of day to visit properties is around dinnertime, before dark, on any working day. If you go on the weekends, visit either on a Saturday morning, or late on a Sunday afternoon, when property owners are more likely to be home.

Pause and Examine the House From the Street:

When you get to the house, pause before going to the door so you can evaluate the property. Look closely at the roof and windows. Note if the roof is level and without sags, the condition of the shingles, and whether the window and door openings are square and true. Window and door openings that are twisted out of square are indicators of potentially expensive structural problems.

Now, take a deep breath and then head straight for the door. Make sure that you have nothing in your hands (including a clipboard, file folder, or anything else), because property owners think that people with files and clipboards are either salesmen, fund raisers, or representatives from the bank.

Dress Appropriately for the Job and Match the Door Knocker to the Neighborhood:

Your door-knocker should look as unassuming and unthreatening as possible. Have them wear comfortable, clean clothes, such as khakis and a polo shirt for men and similar basic outfits for women. Tell the door-knockers not to wear a suit, since many people feel intimidated or threatened by people in suits. Match the door-knocker to the neighborhood. For example, if you are sending door knockers to middle class neighborhoods send door-knockers that fit in. This means they are neat and well groomed, speak standard English, and look like people one would expect to meet in the neighborhood.

Further Instructions for Door-Knocking:

If you notice that all the curtains and shades are drawn, that there are no lights on inside and there is debris out in the yard, do not worry. This is normal for a foreclosure or bankruptcy lead. Knock on the door and wait. If the owner is there, he will probably come to the door. He may open it a crack and ask what you want. Tell him you noticed that the house is going up for foreclosure or his bankruptcy is having trouble and that you might be able to help him resolve the problem. If you encounter resistance, try to keep the owner talking for a few minutes. Begin to establish a rapport with him, even if you just chat about how nice the neighborhood is. After you have talked for a while, he will relax and probably let you into the house.

Get into the House:

If the property owner does not want to let you in, ask to use the bathroom, and on your way to the bathroom, take a look around to get an idea of the condition of the house. While you are in the bathroom, notice its condition. A bathroom is an extremely expensive room to renovate, and if it is in poor condition, make a mental note so that you can update the inspection sheet later.

Establish Rapport:

Once you are in the house, sit down with the property owner, wherever they are most comfortable, either in the kitchen or in the living room. If they offer you anything to drink, absolutely accept it. Not accepting an offer of this kind is insulting, and it will make them feel uncomfortable with you. Even if you accept a cup of coffee and do not touch it, or a drink of water and do not drink it, that's fine, just accept their offer. In doing so, you can strengthen your rapport and prolong your visit.

Explain Who You Are and What You Can Offer:

You will find that the property owner is probably defensive and wondering what on earth you can do for them. At the risk of my being too repetitive, you should tell the owner that:

- you are an investor and that you specialize in working out foreclosures and working with homeowners having trouble with their bankruptcy;

- you have looked into their situation after seeing the foreclosure notice or bankruptcy notice on-line;

- you stopped by because you think you may be able to stop the foreclosure or make it so the difficult bankruptcy doesn't matter;

- you can help to preserve their credit and if the foreclosure is stopped, keep it from getting any worse by having a completed foreclosure;

- get them some money in their pocket;

- help them get situated in a new home or apartment

- stop the embarrassment of a public auction of their property;

- eliminate the possibility of the mortgage company pursuing the homeowner for any "deficiency" if the mortgage company does not recover the full loan balance from the sale of the property;

- take care of the past due real estate taxes, lien holders, and mortgage holders; and

- relieve their worries.

Remember: Do Not Lend Money

You will find that most people facing foreclosure are anxious to find any way that they can to borrow money in order to refinance or bring their mortgage up to date. You must tell them

> Follow the famous advice of Ben Franklin as it applies to property owners in foreclosure. "Neither a borrower nor a lender be."

that you are not going to lend them money and that, given their situation, they should not hold out any hopes of borrowing money from someone else with their credit and the foreclosure lawsuit.

Lending money to someone in foreclosure is the express route to lawsuits, so do not do it. The person who owes you money and is unable to pay you back will hate you when you demand they repay the money. They will also be happy to sue you once you go to enforce your rights. Lawsuits are always expensive, unpleasant, and somewhat uncertain. If you want to make money in the foreclosure business, you need to stay out of court as much as possible.

The alternate highway to lawsuits is allowing a former owner to stay in a property which they have sold to you. Other than for a short time such as a few weeks. If you do allow an owner to stay even for a few weeks while they prepare to move. You MUST have a deed from the property owner which you must record and you MUST have a signed lease from the property owner. You must get these documents BEFORE you stop the foreclosure. The deed will secure your position as the owner without further legal action and the lease will allow you to evict the former owner which is the cheapest and simplest method to get a property owner out of the property.

Be aware that there are valid legal theories which can make it so that a property owner can keep their house or stay in it for their lifetime even though you have bought the house and paid for it. These lawsuits are much less likely to be brought up and much less likely to be successful if you followed my advice. In a nutshell, that advice is:

- Never lend money to anyone in foreclosure or bankruptcy;

- Do not allow the property owner to stay in the house other than for a very short time while they prepare to move;

- Do not stop the foreclosure sale or give significant money to anyone until you have a signed deed and lease from the property owner; and

- Do not agree to resell the property to the person in the future. This can make you susceptible to usury claims, lending law violations, fraud claims, and lawsuits under the many state laws that regulate the foreclosure business (including, but not limited to California, Minnesota, Maryland, Illinois, New York, etc.).

Be firm and consistent with the property owner. Make it clear to the property owner that if you are going to help them, it is going to be on your terms.

Those terms are that they will get money to help them move into a new place, they will get a new clean, safe place to live, but they must leave the house that they currently live in and cannot afford.

Gather Information:

Take a foreclosure information sheet and suggested questions from your pocket and fill it in as you go over the situation with the property owners. Find out from them what debts exist against the property and approximately what each of the balances are. Keep in mind that property owners in this situation do not usually know the correct balance on their loans. You must always check up on everything. Do not commit to any offer to the property owner until you have verified all liens and lien balances.

Be sure to have the owner give you the various lien holder names, addresses and account numbers. Have them sign a letter of permission allowing the lien holder to talk to you about the debt. (See the forms package for a blank.)

Keep Expectations Low:

Make sure that you keep the property owners' expectations low. Ideally, you want to simply give them enough money to move to another place. The benefits to the property owner of selling is an end to the stress of foreclosure and bankruptcy problems. You will stop the foreclosure which will save them embarrassment, pay off their loans to stop any potential deficiency judgments, and help them get a fresh start in a nice new apartment or rental house. Point out that renting a house in the same neighborhood is probably 1/3 less expensive than owning and they do not have to worry about unexpected repairs and they can close out the stressful foreclosure and bankruptcy period of their lives.

Avoid Renting to Former Owners or Tenants:

I have almost never seen a situation where former property owners or tenants will ever pay rent to a new owner. If you do purchase a house that is occupied, be ready to take action quickly if the occupant does not pay rent.

Sometimes you need to rent to the property owner to make a deal. Never do this for a long-term solution. Limit rentals to ninety days. You will need to decide for yourself if the particular property owner is likely to cause you a heap of trouble if you have to evict them. My advice is that it is almost inevitable that the occupant will not pay, you need to budget money for an ejectment or an eviction action. A typical cost for an ejectment in Pennsylvania is $7,000, compared to $900 for an eviction. In addition, it will probably take a number of months for you to physically force the owner from the property. Make sure you build that cost and extra holding costs into your purchase cost. If you get them out at more quickly, or if they pay it will just be additional profit for you.

The Show

I was speaking to an investor with about twenty years experience in foreclosures about closing the deal with a property owner. Investor "X" as I will call him has a show for the homeowners, complete with props. Investor "X" 's props are a deed, a lease and ten crisp $100 bills. He takes out the deed, the lease and the bills. He tells the homeowner once they sign the deed and lease, they can have the $100 bills. These are cash starved people. They jump at the chance to have ten crisp $100 bills. All the homeowner needs to do is sign the papers and he gives them the cash. I think Investor "X" has a good idea for low income, unsophisticated owners. You may consider using his idea next time you visit that kind of a homeowner in foreclosure ready to close a deal. Do not try this technique with more sophisticated homeowners.

Give Money Only After You Have the Signed Lease and Deed:

Make it clear to the property owner that you will give them whatever money you agree to give them after they have signed a deed and lease or occupancy agreement, not before. If they ask you for money to make a down payment on an apartment, tell them that you will be happy to meet with their new landlord and turn over the deposit directly to that landlord.

No money should be given until you have a signed deed to the property and a signed lease. If they want money to rent a truck, meet them at the truck rental agency. Let them rent the truck in their name and hand the cash directly over the counter to the rental agent. Do not put the damage deposit on your credit card or do anything else that will make you responsible for the truck.

Do not ever give the property owner any money directly if you expect that money to go to rent a truck, apartment or anywhere other than to the property. Property owners in foreclosure are really starved for cash. They have so many needs crying out for cash that if you give them any, it will likely not go to moving expenses as agreed, but rather to some other pressing need (i.e., car repair, school tuition, most obnoxious creditor, etc.).

Do Not Agree to Sell the Property Back to the Property Owner:

I have seen many situations where property owners have made an agreement with the investor that they will stay in the house and pay rent and then buy the house back again in the future. These agreements end badly. Almost all property owners in foreclosure want to buy their house back again. Keep in mind that people are creatures of habit. In a case of someone whose property is in foreclosure, that means they will just repeat their previous pattern of non-payment. You want to avoid being the next creditor that does not get paid. This arrangement can also cause you to run afoul of usury and lending laws as well as the newer laws controlling investors such as the New

York, California, Minnesota, Maryland, and Illinois.

If you are going to agree to let the property owner stay for any period of time, insist that they sign the deed over to you and that they sign a lease. Consult with your attorney prior to signing a lease with any owner. In many states (New York, California, Massachusetts, New Jersey) you may have trouble terminating the lease. A lease is a fairly strong document that will allow you to evict them, if they do not pay. Property owners that are being evicted from their homes tend to be vindictive, and it is very likely that they will damage your house before they leave. For all of the above reasons, I really prefer that you get them out of your house, even if you have to pay money for them to rent another house. Once the property owner is physically out of the house, you are much less likely to have any future problems with them. Mentally, they leave the whole thing behind, and they do not want to go back to the house because it brings up very painful memories.

Stay in Control:

You must stay in control of the situation. You do this by staying in control of the money and by keeping the pressure on the property owner such that if he does not do what he promised, he will lose the house to foreclosure and dealing with you will not solve any of his problems. These are people who often wait until the last second to act. If you stop the foreclosure clock from ticking before he has followed through, the property owner will go back to his normal mode of operating which is to ignore problems, refuse to pay, and fail to keep up with obligations and commitments. He will not act until another emergency comes up. That emergency will typically be the house being rescheduled for sheriff's sale.

Do not cause the foreclosure sale to be postponed or "stayed" (stopped) until the property owner signs the deed over to you and signs a lease or moves out. It may take many months to schedule a new foreclosure sale. By then, the financial picture of this foreclosure may change to the extent that it is not profitable.

Finalize the Deal with a Deed:

Once you have struck a deal with the property owner, schedule a settlement or simply have him sign a deed over to you. You need to be sure that all the people who own the house, including current spouses, even if they are not named on the deed, sign the deed and thereby transfer the house over to you. At the time they sign the deed, you may consent to give them some money, such as $500, but save most of the

> ### Be Prepared for the Last Minute Pre-Foreclosure Deal
>
> Keep in mind that property owners in foreclosure have failed to act to solve their money problem for a long time leading up to the foreclosure sale. Don't expect this Zebra to change his stripes!
>
> He will continue to ignore his problems until the foreclosure sale is upon him.
>
> Do not be surprised if the property owner is only receptive to making a deal in the last days leading to the foreclosure sale.

money for when they vacate the house. It may help to motivate the sellers to sign if you have cash ready to hand them once they sign the deed.

Using a deed signed in front of a notary is a very informal settlement and should be done only by an experienced investor. If you are not completely confident of your ability to read the title report, fill in a HUD-1 and deed, and hold a settlement, use an attorney or title company to conduct settlement. The reason you may be tempted to hold an informal settlement is that the owner has delayed so long that it is the eve of a foreclosure sale when you finally work out a deal. Do not let his irresponsibility force you to act irresponsibly. Be sure to get a title report and title insurance or the approval of a competent attorney before you lay out a lot of money.

Have the Deed Professionally Drafted:

On your first deals, you will have to get your attorney or title company involved in the process so that they can draw up the deed for you. Since these deeds can be contested, you will need to make sure they are drawn up properly. Deeds are not very expensive documents to have drawn up. They average approximately $125 in my area. As you get close to putting a deal together, call your attorney and have him draw up a deed for you so that you will be prepared. As soon as you obtain the agreement from the property owners, have them immediately sign the deed in front of a notary. Do not procrastinate; the property owners may change their minds or try to shop for a better deal. Once they sign the deed and give it to you, you own the property and they can no longer change their minds.

If you are holding an informal or formal settlement, be sure the property owners sign my disclosures stating that they know they are selling you the house so they do not later deny knowing what they were doing. The disclosure forms are on the forms disk.

Do not agree to resell the house to the property owner at a higher price or you may run afoul of usury laws. A court could also decide you made an illegally secured loan rather than a sale. In some states such as New York, there is a law that states sales from the homeowner to you with an agreement to resell the home to the owner in the future is a loan transaction. In either event no good will come of it.

If you need to offer the property owner the chance to buy back the house in order to make a deal, offer to sell the property owner the property at fair market value any time over the next two years or at some pre-designated discount from fair market value. Sign an agreement that fair market value will be established by hiring an independent appraiser. The appraiser will do an appraisal and come up with the fair market value which is what the property owner will pay you to buy back the house. Do not set a specific price up front.

Once you have finalized your deal with the property owner, move quickly to finish whatever dealings you plan to have with the lenders and lien holders. If you are going to reinstate the loan, contact the attorney for the lender and make those arrangements. If you are going to purchase mortgages at a discount, finalize those purchases.

A Partner Can Make Dealing With Property Owners Easier:

Some people find that it is useful to tell people that they have a partner, whether they do or not. That way, it is easier to play good guy/bad guy. You can say something like, "Gee, I would really love to agree to that, but my partner will not let me." If the property owner knows that everything is up to you, once you get friendly and establish a rapport, the property owner will start asking you for favors. An imaginary hard-bargaining partner can make it easier to say "no." Imagine yourself saying "I'd love to help you out, but my partner will not agree to that."

No matter what method you use, be firm with the property owner. Remember that this is a business transaction and that you cannot be too flexible, otherwise, you will lose money. Live up to your part of the bargain and demand that they live up to theirs, too.

Calculating Your Offer:

When you are deciding how much to offer the property owner, start out low. Figure out the most you could pay using my "flipper" or "rental" spreadsheet. Those spreadsheets are on your forms disk. Try to offer just enough money for the owner to move out and get a new place to live.

Do not share your math with the property owner. Do not tell the property owner that you will purchase any of their loans at a discount. Keep in mind that your goal is to buy the house as inexpensively as possible, and that every extra dollar you spend represents both additional risk and less profit. Make offers to the property owner phrased as "I will give you $3,000 once the house is vacant" rather than "I will give you $18,000 for the house." This keeps the homeowner focused on the amount they will actually receive rather than the sale price.

Use the spreadsheets included on the forms disk to help you calculate your offer. If you are buying the house as a rental property, make sure that there will be a positive cash flow of and if you are buying to flip be sure there is enough profit. The "rentals" and "flipper" spreadsheets are outstanding tools that you should get used to using.

Sell Your Deal by Presenting It as a Solution to the Property Owner's Problems:

Property owners in foreclosure are problem-focused, not money-focused. Sell the property owner on the point that you will take care of this headache for them. I can guarantee you that this foreclosure has been keeping these people up many nights, twisting and turning and depriving them of sleep. If they are failing bankruptcy, then the homeowner feels frustrated and disgusted. What you are offering the property owner is relief from worry. Tell them you can get them their money very quickly and get them into a new house, so they will not have to worry about this problem anymore. That will appeal to them, even if they are not getting as much money as they would like to get for the house. Here again are some selling points:

You can:

- give them money to put down on an apartment and pay to move;
- stop the foreclosure and the embarrassment of having their house sold at public auction;
- stop them from having to make those high bankruptcy payments each month;
- prevent their name from being published in the paper again;
- make the best of their credit situation (this will help them buy a house in the future);
- take care of the loans against the house;
- stop the harassment of the lien holders and mortgage lenders;
- prevent the possibility of a deficiency judgment; and
- help them get a FRESH START away from their worries.

Do Not Get Involved in Fights
With Property Owners:

You want to make a deal with the property owner to avoid an adversarial situation. Adversarial situations are generally money losing propositions. I think lending or entering into a situation where you are likely to get into a dispute with the homeowner (such as renting the property back to them where they may default on the rent payment) or any long term business relationship is a big mistake. You will end up spending lots of time and money, being aggravated and not making the profit you expected when you became involved.

Section Four

Technical Matters

8

Estimating the Value
of Properties

In order to make money buying and selling real estate, you must know
how much the property is worth in its current condition and how much
you will be able to sell the property for once it has been repaired. This
chapter outlines various methods you can use to estimate the value of a piece
of property. You must understand the information in this chapter, or you
will not be able to calculate how much you can afford to pay for a piece of
property and still make a profit when you resell it.

The Comparable Sales Method

The first method we will examine is called the Comparable Sales Method.
We will discuss this method first because it is the method I generally recommend for estimating the retail value of a house you are planning to buy,
repair, and resell.

The comparable sales method involves finding three or more similar houses
in the neighborhood which have sold within the past six months. The hous-

es should be similar in type of neighborhood, size, construction, and condition. Ideally, they should all have been sold through a real estate agent. The fundamental idea is that your house will be worth about the same as similar houses recently sold in the neighborhood. Your job is to find similar houses which have sold recently.

Real estate will bring different prices depending upon how it is marketed. You should use as "comparables" those properties which were sold in the same way you plan to sell your property. You should not use as comparables any properties sold as part of a package called a "blanket sale," sold at a foreclosure sale, at auction, as part of an estate, or in some other unusual way unless you plan on re-selling the property using that method.

If you do not have access to recent property sale information, you must find it. You can look on the internet at Zillow.com or you can ask a real estate agent or appraiser to run you a list of "comparables." Another method is to go to the public real estate records in your county and check for recent sales in the neighborhood. When properties are sold, a paper called a "deed" is drafted which is brought to the county courthouse and recorded in the county records. The deed contains the names of the old and new owner and the selling price. The records are accessible to the public. You will be able to obtain price information from these deeds. You must look at each property you think is a potential "comparable"!

Comparable Sales Analysis Example

Address	Selling Price	Days on Market	Sale Date	Notes
2750 N. 47th St.	$50,000	366	7/98	3 Bdrm Row, 1 Bath Smaller, Newer
2719 N. 47th St.	$57,900	302	2/98	3 Bdrm Row, 1 Bath
2714 N. 47th St.	$69,900	196	5/98	Small 3 Bdrm, Newer Construction
2737 N. 47th St.	$64,500	185	5/98	House Next Door,
Average =	$60,575	262		Identical size

Explanation: The house I was trying to estimate the value for was located at 2739 North 47th Street. These houses were all sales on the block in 1998. The two houses with odd addresses, 2737 and 2719, were almost identical houses to the subject house. They were all built around 1941 and were the same size with the same number of bathrooms and bedrooms. The average price of 2719 and 2737 was $61,200. The average time to sell the houses was 243 days. I decided the subject house was worth in the low $60,000's ($60,000-$65,000). It eventually sold for $63,000.

The Asking Price Method: An alternative method to estimate the value of a property is to drive through a neighborhood, write down the phone numbers on the for sale signs, and call the real estate agent for the asking price. On average, houses sell for about 6% less than their asking price. If you are using the asking price method, discount the price by 6% before using the home as a guideline for prices. Do not use "for sale by owner" properties to estimate value. For sale by owner properties tend to be wildly mis-priced.

Be aware that the "asking price - 6%" method is not as reliable as basing your estimate on houses which have actually sold in the recent past. Use it when you want to get a rough idea of the value of a particular piece of property. Get more reliable information before investing any money in a particular property.

Asking Price Method Example If I were to use the asking price method to estimate the value of the house at 2739 North 47th Street, the numbers would look like this:

Address	Selling Price	Days on Market	Notes
2713 N. 46th St.	$65,000	75	Same House, Better Street
2756 N. 46th St.	$65,500	102	Same House, Better Street
2733 N. 45th St.	$69,900	75	Same House, Quiet Street
4412 Sherwood Rd.	$69,900	78	Same House, Better Yard, Better Street
Average =	$67,575	82	

Explanation: If we used the "asking price minus 6%" method, my estimate of value would have been $63,500. If I removed the house on Sherwood Road from the analysis because of the better block, yard and street, my estimate would have been 6% less than the average asking price of $66,800 which would be $62,972. Interesting how well this worked out. I sold 2739 N. 47th Street for $63,000!

Other Methods of Estimating the Value of Real Estate

There are other methods which are used to estimate the value of property. The two most popular are the "cash flow" method and the "replacement cost" method. The cash flow method should be used for rental properties and the replacement cost method should generally only be used by you for determining how much insurance you need to carry on the building.

The Cash Flow Method: (For Rental Property) This method of estimating value involves determining how much money would be generated each month if the property were to be rented out. This method does not indicate the sale value of a particular property unless the property is going to be sold to an investor for use as a rental. If you are considering the purchase of a multi unit apartment building, commercial building, or some other income-producing property, the cash flow method is the best method to indicate the value. There is a computerized spreadsheet in my forms set to help you perform this analysis. Instructions are in the spreadsheet itself.

The spreadsheet that produced the output in the next exhibit is included with the forms set.

The Replacement Cost Method: This method values a property on the basis of how much it would cost to rebuild the property today. This is useful if you want to know how much fire/hazard insurance to purchase on your property. It generally has little to do with what any particular person might pay for your property, or with what you should pay for a property.

Remember, for the purpose of calculating how much a piece of property will be worth when you sell it, the value that matters is how much a buyer will pay you for that property, which is directly related to how much similar properties cost in the area or how much rental income a rental property can generate. The replacement cost does not usually indicate what a retail buyer will pay for a property, because the retail buyer is usually choosing between your property and other similar properties on the market. The retail buyer's alternatives are which finished property to buy, not whether to buy your property or build his own.

The replacement cost method can be used to value unique properties where no comparable properties exist. An example would be a football stadium, factory, or some other property which has no competition on the market because there are no similar properties. This is not relevant to this course because I do not suggest that you invest in unique properties until and unless you have many years of experience in the real estate business. Unique properties can be difficult to market, which means that they can take a long time to sell. It can also be difficult to accurately estimate the price at which you will ultimately sell your unique property. This lack of information makes it difficult to know how much you can pay for a property and still realize a profit. All of these factors increase the riskiness of involving yourself with unique properties.

For the above reasons, you should not use the replacement cost method other than for the purpose of estimating how much insurance you will need. If you feel that you need to use this method, hire a professional appraiser to employ the method for you.

Be Conservative in Valuing Property

Whenever you are estimating property values, regardless of the method you use, be conservative. By "conservative" I mean that, given a choice between two likely alternatives, you should always choose the lower value for the property being analyzed. In this way, if you are wrong, you will make more money rather than lose money. It is better not to participate in a potential transaction then to guess and hope with your hard-earned money.

Remember to Evaluate the Saleability of the Neighborhood: If you are buying to "Flip" a property, it is important that you evaluate how quickly you will be able to resell the property. Some of the factors which tend to make a neighborhood one in which houses sell quickly are: the neighborhood is one that people are moving into (you can determine by checking on whether prices in the area have been increasing or decreasing over the past few years); there is new construction of housing and shopping going on in the area; new public transportation, highways, or other public infrastructure are being added that will bring people into the area; and new employers are springing up, or existing employers are expanding in the local area. You can also judge the sale-ability of a neighborhood by the number of "for sale" signs in a neighborhood. Too many signs usually means slow-moving neighborhood. This is because the houses for sale have "backed up" in the market because houses are not selling quickly.

When you are trying to learn about a neighborhood, ask residents of the neighborhood, real estate agents, and other investors.

Real estate agents keep a lot of useful statistics. The computer system the real estate agents use to list properties for sale is called the "Multiple Listing System" or "MLS." Most of the MLS systems keep track of the number of days that a property is on the market before it is sold or withdrawn, which will typically be identified with the initials D.O.M. ("days on market"). Take a look at the number of days the typical property is on the market. For planning purposes, estimate that, once it is fixed up, your property will be on the market for at least that length of time. You will, of course, use the marketing techniques discussed elsewhere in this book along with your common sense, and buyer incentives, to turn over this property as quickly as possible.

Is the Property in a Fast or Slow Moving Market?

Time Needed to Sell	Saleability Rating
Less than 46 days	Fast selling neighborhood
46-90 days	Average selling neighborhood
More than 90 days	Slow selling neighborhood

Note: Be sure to compare the marketing time for properties which are similar to yours. Commercial properties in the same neighborhood sell at a different rate from Residential property.

If you plan to purchase a house in a slow-moving neighborhood, calculate additional holding costs for the longer marketing period. Deduct the additional holding costs from what you are willing to pay for the property.

Holding Costs: Whenever you are evaluating an investment property, you must always consider holding costs. Holding costs are your costs to own the real estate between the time you buy it and the time you sell it. These costs include taxes, insurance, maintenance, and utility bills. The flipper spreadsheet in m Investor's Essentials forms set does this for you automatically.

Analysis Paralysis: You will never have complete information when you buy property. Leave some "room" in your calculations for unplanned repairs and some mis-calculation on your part. If you feel uncomfortable with a particular deal, increase your margin for error by paying less.

The effect of demanding a greater discount is that you will have to shop longer to find a deal. You may not be able to buy cheaply unless you use one of the advanced techniques. The advanced techniques include buying liens and mortgages at a discount, buying pre-foreclosures, out of bankruptcy, negotiating with the IRS and other creditors.

I teach those techniques in my home study courses and live seminars. Look at www.bobdiamondrealestate.com or call us at 800-608-0514.

9

What Kind of Properties Should You Invest In?

There are many types of real estate that you can invest in. The different types include vacant land, single family homes, apartment buildings, storage garages, offices, commercial, and industrial space.

For an investor such as yourself, there are significant differences between the various types of property. The best investments for most beginning and small investors are what I call "single dwellings," small apartment buildings (up to four units), and storage garages. Unless you have other experience in real estate, you should stick to these types of properties.

The balance of this chapter is devoted to discussing specifically the various types of property available and the advantages and disadvantages of each.

Single Dwellings

Single dwellings are my favorite type of property for the small investor. I include within the definition of a single dwelling stand-alone houses (called "single family homes") and properties which are attached side to side in groups of two or more B sometimes called "twins," "townhouses," or "rowhouses." This definition does not include buildings in which living units are stacked one on top of another. I call those multi-unit buildings. The definition also does not include condominiums, which are discussed separately.

Single dwellings are easy to sell or rent. More people are interested in purchasing and renting this type of housing than any other. The popularity of a single dwelling will protect you from extended vacancy for rental units and from long periods of waiting for a property to sell.

Single dwellings tend to attract the best qualified tenants, whose income and living situations are most stable. You should therefore have less trouble collecting rent, fewer vacancies, and less demand on your time to actively manage the property.

It has been my experience that single dwellings tend to stay occupied by the same tenants for several years before they move out. Apartment renters move much more often. For small apartments, such as efficiencies, tenants move most frequently. Vacancy and turnover costs which include cleaning, repainting, repairing, and advertising are very expensive to a landlord in terms of both time and money. Turnover costs typically equal at least one and one-half to two months' rent on a property. Single dwellings minimize turnover and thereby minimize the costs to you in terms of your money and your time.

I also like single dwellings for investment because it is relatively simple to evaluate how much money you will be able to sell or rent the property for. Houses in neighborhoods tend to be similar in size and amenities and therefore sell and rent for similar prices. This is in contrast to a commercial property (office, store, or other business-use space) where estimating market value and rents can be more difficult.

Summary: In summary, single dwellings are generally good investments because:

- you have a large market of people to whom you can sell or rent;
- it is easy to determine rental and sale value;
- the houses sell or rent quickly;
- you can attract great tenants; and
- they are easy to manage.

Examples of "Single Dwellings"

Single Family House
One type of "Single Dwelling"

Twin Homes
Another type of "Single Dwelling"

Row Homes/Townhomes
Another type of "Single Dwelling"

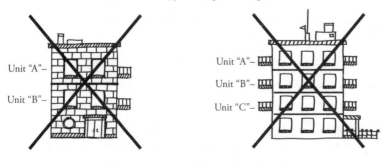

These **are not** "Single Dwellings"

Storage Garages

Garages used as storage space are also one of my favorite kinds of rental properties. Storage garages tend to rent out very quickly, have very few management headaches, and demand very little maintenance. If you are buying to flip, storage garages are saleable but the market for them is smaller than the market for single dwellings. You will have to manage the garages while attempting to sell them.

Rental Garages Are Inexpensive to Erect and Maintain: They are very simple and often lack plumbing, heating, and sometimes even electricity. This minimizes the cost to build and maintain them.

It is Easy to Evict if Necessary: Landlord/tenant laws tend to be more liberal for storage space than they are for dwelling units, so if tenants do not pay, it is usually easier to get rid of their belongings than it would be if the unit were a residence.

How to Analyze a Rental Garage: If you are evaluating a garage as an investment, start first with an income property analysis sheet and use that to estimate the monthly cash flow. Next, use a comparable sales analysis to estimate the value of the land and buildings. Rely primarily on the method which matches your plan for the property. Remember to estimate rents and comparable sales from similar facilities only. Rent is highest for storage space which is enclosed within a fence and benefits from 24-hour on-site security.

Be Aware of What is Being Stored in Your Garages: Be careful that people do not store flammable or hazardous materials inside the units. Include in the lease a statement that the tenant will not be permitted to store flammables (such as paint), explosives (such as gasoline), any other volatile compounds, or any other hazardous wastes, on your site. You need to be very firm about hazardous wastes because if there is a spill on your site, you will have to pay for the cleanup. You may not ever get reimbursed by the person who spilled the substance at your property. In addition, if someone is storing flammable or volatile compounds, it greatly increases the risk of fire or other calamities, which may destroy your garages. Make it a practice to keep your eye on what is stored in the garages.

Investigate the Rental Market Before You Buy: Before you invest in rental garages, investigate whether or not the market is saturated with rental space. Check the paper for garage space being offered for rent and call the landlords and talk to them. The best areas for rental garages tend to be in and around cities, areas with universities, areas with large concentrations of apartments, military installations, and other areas where large numbers of people move in and out frequently.

Summary: In summary, garages can be terrific investments, because they are cheap to build and maintain, rent out easily, and will demand a relatively small amount of your time to manage. In addition, there is little liability from serious and generally uninsurable risks such as lead base paint poisoning, asbestos, and other environmental problems. The cautions are for you to check what people are storing in your garages, investigate whether there is a market of people looking to rent garage space in your area, and to be aware that this is a project better suited as a rental rather than to buy and immediately resell.

Multi-Unit Buildings

Cash Flow Example Single Swellings Compared to Multi-Unit Dwellings		
	Single Dwelling	Multi-Unit
Monthly Rental Income	$750	$1,300
Monthly Mortgage & Ins. Payment	(385)	(525)
Monthly Taxes	(150)	(175)
Vacancy	(39)	(88)
Repairs	(52)	(88)
Utilities	(0)	(100)
Net Gross Monthly Cash Flow	$124	$324

Single Dwellings Compared to Multi-Unit Dwellings

Single Dwelling

Benefits:
- Easiest to manage
- Many buyers when you resell
- More potential tenants want to rent single dwellings
- Tenants usually stay for the longest duration
- Easiest to estimate rental and sale value
- Easiest to resell
- Tenant takes care of grass, sidewalks, driveways
- Tenant pays for ALL utilities
- More likely to appreciate in value over time
- Tenants tend not to call you for every little repair

Drawbacks:
- More roofs, heaters, etc. to maintain
- Less cash flow
- Each unit costs more than a multi-family unit

Multi-Unit Dwelling

Benefits:
- Better monthly cash flow
- Less risk - not a total loss of income when a unit is vacant
- Income while you wait for property to sell
- Possible condominium conversion

Drawbacks:
- Tenants move more often
- Landlord must resolve Fights/ Disputes between tenants
- Common areas to take care of
- Common utilities to pay for
- More of your time to manage
- Need more repairs due to tenants moving in and out more often and tenants which tend to be harder on the units
- Harder to resell

Multi unit buildings include duplexes (two units stacked one on top of the other), triplexes (three units stacked on top of each other), and apartment buildings.

Small multi-units are great starter investments. You need to carefully screen your tenants by checking credit, calling references and being observant, but the cash flow can be great. If you want to learn how to do landlording, I have a course available. Call my office at 800-608-0514 for more information.

Multi family properties can be very attractive because their cost-per-unit is lower than the cost-per-unit for a single dwelling. Even though the cost per unit is lower, the rents you collect per unit for multi-family properties are not proportionately less than for single dwellings. Be sure to use the analysis spreadsheet included in my Investor's Essentials forms set to calculate your cash flows.

The same number of living units configured as part of a multi-unit will usually be a little more profitable than the same number of living units configured as single dwellings. The cost to the landlord is more management time and effort to manage the multi-unit as well as having an investment that is harder to resell.

Apartment Dwellers Tend to be Less Desirable Tenants: My experience has been that multi-unit apartment dwellers seem to have less stable jobs and family situations, leading to a higher rate of default on rental payments and more frequent turnover. In addition, I have found that those renters tend to be less self sufficient and harder on the rental unit. This means that you will get telephone calls for jammed garbage disposals, clogged up pipes, and disputes between tenants that you will not get nearly so often with a single dwelling. In addition, you need to arrange for someone to take care of the common areas of the multi family unit, which would include common hallways, basements, sidewalks and lawns. Also, you will probably have to be responsible for some of the utilities, including water, sewer, and any other utility not regulated on a separate meter.

Multi-Units Have Better Cash Flow: The cash flow from a multi unit building will usually be higher than the cash flow from the same number of single dwelling units. In part, this is because your maintenance costs per unit on a single dwelling tends to be higher because each single dwelling has its own roof, heater, sewer, etc.

Multi-Units Take More Time to Manage: A drawback to owning multi unit buildings is the additional time that you will spend managing the multi unit property as compared to the time you would spend managing the same number of units of single dwellings.

Multi-Units are Harder to Finance: It can be difficult to finance some multi family dwellings. Most loan programs through banks and other traditional mortgage lenders will only allow financing of a residential property which is four units or less in configuration. Once you are above four units under one roof, the financing generally needs to be custom financing, which is negotiated between the borrower and the lender for that particular loan. Lenders are comfortable lending 65 – 70% of the purchase price. It can be very costly in terms of loan fees and down payment requirements to get commercial financing. The interest you will be paying will usually be higher than it would be for a loan for a property of four units or less. If you are evaluating multi-units for investment call a few banks to check on rates and fees.

Multi-Units Are Harder to Re-Sell: Multi-unit properties, which include any property where living units are stacked on top of one another, are harder to sell. The buyers are generally limited to investors. A small multi-unit of up to four units may be purchased by an enterprising retail buyer. The buyer may be able to live in one apartment, manage the rest, and have the rent he collects cover the mortgage. There are not that many enterprising retail buyers out there.

Multi-units of five to forty units are odd balls. They are too large for an enterprising retail buyer, yet too small for large investors. These properties sell very slowly, the market is limited to local small-time investors who are trying to expand, and the owner usually has to finance a portion of the sale. I have had great success in this niche.

Multi-units over forty units are usually bought by larger local and national investors. These investors are professional property managers. Beginning investors are not qualified or competent to handle these properties.

If you plan to flip the multi family building, you should allocate more time, more holding costs, and higher advertising costs to the selling effort. Renting some or all of the units while you are marketing the building will probably offset the holding costs, but you will have to spend your time managing the property while it is up for sale.

Summary: Multi-units provide better cash flow at the expense of more management time and effort on the owner's part. They are harder to sell, finance, and manage than single dwellings. The small multi-unit is simple enough for a small investor to manage but the initial analysis should be done in consultation with an experienced professional (appraiser or real estate agent with a "CCIM" designation) or another experienced investor. If you have the necessary experience, use the spreadsheets to help you.

Vacant Land

Vacant land is generally not good for a small investor for two reasons: first, you cannot usually generate income from it until you have spent time, effort, and money to build upon the property; second, the market of buyers and users of vacant land is smaller. This will make it harder for you to sell or rent the land. Longer marketing time will result in higher costs and lower profits. You are also likely to have higher Real Estate Agent's commissions and advertising costs due to the longer marketing period.

Developing Vacant Land is Expensive and Uncertain: The work involved in building upon raw land can be time-consuming and expensive. Such work includes obtaining approvals to build, hiring architects and engineers to lay out the building plans, obtaining building permits, soliciting bids from contractors, financing, and overseeing the construction. This can take many months and thousands of dollars. If you are trying to use the land for a purpose for which it has not been currently approved, such as building townhouses on land zoned or approved for single family homes, you will have to go through governmental proceedings to gain the approval. You will need to hire architects, engineers and attorneys to represent you in these matters. You may never obtain your approvals, and you would be unable to recover those costs.

It is difficult to generate income from vacant land to defray your costs associated with the land. Vacant land can generally not be rented, unless your land can be farmed, used for parking, or storage. Unless the land you are looking at can be put to one of those uses, do not count on generating income from the property until you sell it.

Summary: In summary, vacant land is too complicated, time-consuming, and uncertain to be appropriate for a new investor. For all of the above reasons, consider any type of purchase of vacant land with extreme reluctance. Focus your efforts on simpler, faster projects.

Office Buildings and Commercial Space

Office buildings and commercial space can be good investments under the right circumstances. Commercial and office space leases are often what is called "triple net." This means that the tenant pays for taxes, insurance, and the maintenance on the property.

From the Landlord's perspective, management on these types of properties, once they are rented with good tenants, tends to be minimal requiring not much more than collecting a rent check and depositing it each month. Since tenants are responsible for maintenance, they should not be calling you very often.

The disadvantage of renting office and commercial space is that the market of potential buyers and the supply of renters is usually smaller than the rental or resale market for residential units. If an area is saturated with commercial space, or your space is outdated, your commercial space may never rent.

If you are considering purchasing commercial property, you need to do a careful analysis of the strength of the rental market, the competitive space available, and the rental value of your space. You are much more likely to be successful if you are in a growing area such as Phoenix or Last Vegas, than if you are in an area which is contracting or not growing. Office space can go vacant for extended periods of time, and you must do a careful analysis to be sure that you will not be stuck with an unrentable property. Professional assistance is available from appraisers and real estate agents and you should use their services.

Condominiums

I do not generally recommend investing in condominium units for rental. The monthly maintenance fee tends to eat up whatever positive cash flow would ordinarily come out of the property and the properties do not usually appreciate in value. Typically, the landlord gets stuck paying for things that the tenants would pay for, or do themselves, if the condominium fee did not include the service or utility. These items include such services as shoveling snow, lawn cutting, landscaping, water, sewer, and trash removal. Condo fees for these services, plus outside maintenance, can easily run hundreds of dollars per month. Thus, condos are more expensive to own.

The rent you will receive on a condominium tends to be the same as the market rent on a similar size living space that is not a condominium. Even when I have pointed out to tenants that they are getting additional services with a condominium (i.e., water and sewer, snow removal, grass-cutting) as compared to renting a house, the tenants do not want to pay extra.

Chapter Summary: My favorite kinds of investment properties for new investors are single dwellings and garages. I also endorse the purchase of multi family units, provided that you can tolerate the management nuisances involved. I suggest that a new investor stick with small properties at first, which would include rental garages in groups of six or less, multi family properties of four units or less, single family homes, and attached dwellings.

I recommend these types of investment properties because they are easy to analyze, easy to manage, and there is a large market of renters and purchasers for them. Investing in these types of properties will increase your likelihood of success in real estate investing.

New Investors should invest in:
- Single dwellings;
- Storage garages;
- Small apartment buildings (up to four units, sometimes called "multi-family units');
- Properties within half an hour of your home;
- Small commercial (groups of four stores or less).

Avoid:
- Vacant land;
- Condominiums;
- Large multi-unit buildings;
- Large commercial (strip malls, more than four unit groups).

Expensive versus Inexpensive Properties:

If you can raise the money, larger deals may be better for you. A few larger deals will take less of your time than many small deals. It will usually require the same amount of time on your part to fix up a $30,000 property, as it would a $300,000 one.

If you have time but not as much money or borrowing ability, small transactions can still work for you. There is money to be made in small deals. Sometimes better percentage discounts can be obtained in small deals to increase your percentage profitability.

Where your success lies depends upon your financial situation and which houses you are comfortable with. I suggest you look at your finances, analyze each deal individually, and pursue the deals you are comfortable with. If you are very short of time but have money, pursue large deals. If you have time but not a lot of money, pursue smaller deals.

10

What Neighborhoods Should You Invest In?

Location Controls Maximum and Minimum Value

If you ask most real estate professionals what they consider to be the biggest determinant of value, you will hear one answer: "location, location, location." This is true. The physical location of your property will determine its maximum sale price, rental value, and how quickly it will sell or rent. If you are in an area where a typical house costs $100,000, it is unlikely that any home which is similar in living space or usefulness to other homes in the neighborhood would be worth more than $115,000 or any less than $80,000. Like magnetism, the average price of real estate in the area tends to pull the value of each and every house towards that average.

> The location of a property is the strongest determinant of the value of that property. Do not fight this rule by over-improving property!

If You are Investing in Rental Properties Buy in Modestly Priced Working-Class Neighborhoods: If you consult with knowledgeable real estate investors and experts about where to buy rental properties, you will often be advised to invest in housing in working-class neighborhoods. Working class neighborhoods are those where people such as policemen, firemen, teachers, clerical workers, and assembly line workers live. These tend to be honest, hardworking people who keep their houses in good repair, pay their bills, and make good tenants and neighbors. Houses in working class neighborhoods can be purchased inexpensively and modestly fixed up such that you will receive a positive cash flow on the rental. This is good advice and you should buy in working class neighborhoods if you are investing in rental properties.

Buy Rental Properties in Neighborhoods with Stable or Increasing Values: If you are buying for the purpose of renting it to others, do so in neighborhoods where you believe property values are stable or increasing. This is vital because you plan on owning property for an extended time period. If you are in a declining neighborhood for a long time, you will eventually be stuck with a property which will be unrentable and unsaleable, making it a worthless liability that does nothing more than generate headaches for you.

Neighborhoods with stable or increasing property values can be easily identified. They will have a good reputation, have good access to amenities such as shopping, public transportation, highways, employment, and they appear to be safe. Safe-looking neighborhoods feature well kept lawns and houses, no trash or broken-down cars, no vacant stores or houses, and no people hanging around on corners.

The experts do not recommend investing in rental property in expensive neighborhoods, such as a large single-family home on an acre of ground, because the rent is not high enough to cover the mortgage, taxes, insurance, repairs, and still provide you with a positive cash flow. It is more likely that the property will be have a negative cash flow, meaning that it will cost you money out of your pocket each month that you own the property.

Most real estate experts do not recommend properties at the bottom of the price range (run-down properties typically located in inner city neighborhoods) because the work involved in being a landlord of this type of property is so time-consuming, aggravating, and sometimes dangerous, that few people want the job. This makes the run down properties very hard to resell. Once you buy them, you will be stuck with them.

> **Manners Matter**
> An accurate way to judge the quality of a neighborhood is by the manners of its residents. If the residents are sullen, rude, and generally hostile it is not a good neighborhood and is probably on its way down further.

Whatever price range you choose, try to keep all of your rental properties in one area. Pick an area within half an hour of your home. This will minimize your having to run between properties and will allow you to use the same contractors to fix your properties.

If You are Buying to Flip: If you want to buy properties to flip (properties which you buy, repair and then immediately resell), the factors that you should use in choosing a neighborhood are completely different. When you are buying properties to flip, there are three primary factors to consider:

- how much of a discount can you get on the property (minimum is 20-30% off retail price minus repair costs);
- how quickly the property can be resold; and
- whether or not you can afford the holding costs while waiting for the property to resell.

The best house is the one that fits into your budget and permits you to make a reasonable profit. If you can raise $150,000 to purchase a property, you should probably devote your time to the more expensive properties. If you can only afford less expensive properties, invest in them. Money can also be made on properties bought for $10,000-$15,000, which can be modestly fixed up and then resold for $25,000-$30,000.

More expensive properties produce more income for the same amount of work. A 30% discount off the market price on a $30,000 property is only $9,000. A 30% discount on a $150,000 property is $45,000. The amount of time required to oversee and plan repairs, as well as to actually repair, and resell the properties, is similar whether they are $30,000 or $150,000 properties.

Profitability Comparison between Flipping More/Less Expensive Property: This chart demonstrates the gross profits to be expected from "flipping" properties that vary in cost. Note that the expected profit is about 10% of the retail selling price.

More Expensive Property	Less Mid-Price Property	Inexpensive Property	Item of Property Once Renovated
($210,000)	($91,000)	($21,000)	Investors Purchase Price 70% retail - fix-up)
($18,000)	($3,900)	($0)	Commissions
($3,000)	($1,300)	($300)	Transfer Taxes Paid
($9,000)	($3,900)	($900)	Discount offered to retail buyer (for faster sale)
($2,500)	($1,400)	($750)	Real Estate & School Taxes
($19,500)	($8,450)	($1,950)	Interest Cost to Investor
($1,850)	($900)	($450)	Title Insurance Cost
($600)	($600)	($600)	Insurance ($100/month vacant property policy)
($6,300)	($2,730)	($630)	Other anticipated costs/ contingency reserve
$29,250	$15,820	$3,420	Gross Dollars in Profit

Note: This is a simplified version of the spreadsheet which is included with the computer diskette. The assumptions which generated the numbers shown above are six months to purchase, fix and sell the property, 13% interest on money you borrow, no commission is offered on the inexpensive home because the investor has to do this work to preserve his profit. No repair cost is factored in because it muddies the example. Your profit is not affected so long as you deduct the repair cost form the price you pay for the property.

If you are buying properties to flip, since you are not holding the property for the long term, whether the price of property in the neighborhood is going up, down, or staying the same is not that important. What does matter is that houses on the market in the neighborhood are saleable and move quickly enough for you to sell your property in a reasonable amount of time.

You should investigate and evaluate whether the properties are saleable and

> ### Patience Pays
> In the Philadelphia area, if you are looking at a more expensive home in one of the suburban counties, it would take about three months to locate a bargain property that can be purchased for 30% off.

> ### You Must be Flexible if You Want a Bargain
> If you want a bargain, you must be flexible about the exact style, location, and condition of the property.

if they are selling quickly in the neighborhood. Check the average "days on market" statistic on your multiple listing service. I consider average marketing time forty-five days. If you are buying in a slow selling area, reduce the amount of money you are willing to pay for the property. This will account for the higher holding and advertising costs which are incurred by your owning, maintaining, and advertising the property for a longer time. You will also have an additional cushion enabling you to reduce the price of your house if it does not sell quickly enough.

There are certain neighborhoods where you should be cautious before buying.

One situation is any neighborhood where you would own one of the few houses in a commercial area. A house like that would be difficult to sell or rent. I also do not like nearly new construction in an area where the builder is continuing to build new units. In these neighborhoods, the older housing stock is often called "used housing," and buyers simply do not want it. They prefer a new house where they can pick the carpeting, tile, and counter-tops to suit their tastes, rather than have to accept what is already in your house. Houses that are in neighborhoods still being built up are typically rentable, but it will be hard for you to sell.

HOW TO TELL IF A BAD AREA IS UNDER RENEWAL!

You can tell an area is being renewed if many people are renovating properties in the neighborhood, run down houses are selling quickly to renovators, and the neighborhood is dramatically changing for the better. I look for a neighborhood with a lot of dumpsters.

You do not have to be the first one into a neighborhood to make money rehabilitating houses in a neighborhood undergoing renewal. It usually takes several years for an area to gain momentum and for prices to increase on the run-down properties such that they are not good investments.

If you are involved in real estate investing, you will learn about the neighborhoods in renewal long before the prices go up too much to make the property a good investment. Renewal often starts with government projects to rehabilitate an area. The government funding can jump start private investment in the community.

In all of these situations, a problem property can become a desirable one if the price is low enough. Just make sure to adjust the price you are willing to pay downward to reflect the challenges presented.

Stay Away From Decaying and Run-Down Areas: Beware of any neighborhoods which are run-down and not being improved or gentrified. By "run-down,' I mean neighborhoods with vacant properties, rude residents with little prospect for the future as shown by no investors or homeowners fixing up properties in the neighborhood.

If there are vacant properties in the neighborhood, unless it is a neighborhood which is currently undergoing renewal, it is probably not a place in which you should be buying property. As a general rule, lenders will not lend you or your prospective purchasers any money if there are more than one or two vacant properties on the block.

The Price Range of Properties:

You can make money at all different housing price levels anywhere from a $90,000 attached home in a city to a $400,000 suburban tract home. Where you are able to buy depends on your ability to raise money and pay holding costs while waiting for the property to sell. Where you want to buy depends on other factors such as your available time, risk tolerance, and the housing market in your area.

> **Advice from the Experienced**
> Invest in a particular property only if you can support the taxes, insurance, utilities, and mortgage payment associated with the property for three to six months without additional borrowing. To do otherwise is a recipe for Bankruptcy.

Expensive versus Inexpensive Properties: If you can raise the money, larger deals may be better for you. A few larger deals will take less of your time than many small deals. It will usually require the same amount of time on your part to fix up a $30,000 property, as it would a $300,000 one.

If you have time but not as much money or borrowing ability, small transactions can still work for you. There is money to be made in small deals. Sometimes better percentage discounts can be obtained in small deals to increase your percentage profitability.

Invest Within Your Financial Capabilities: Be sure that you have sufficient income and savings to wait until your house sells. Invest in a property only if you can support the taxes, insurance, utilities, and mortgage payment associated with the property for three to six months without additional borrowing. The money can come from your savings or cash flow from a paycheck, business or other regular source of income. Going into a project without the ability to see it through is a recipe for bankruptcy.

Success Can Be Had at All Price Levels: Investors are successful buying and selling at many price levels, most preferring to buy and sell a greater quantity of less expensive houses. Very few investors I know buy more million dollar houses. These houses are usually ignored by the investors because they cannot raise the money or because they tie up too much money in a single deal. They can be profitable investments if you have the money to buy them.

A problem property can become a desirable one if the price is low enough. Just make sure to adjust the price you are willing to pay downward to reflect the challenges presented.

Where your success lies depends upon your financial situation and which houses you are comfortable with. I suggest you look at your finances, analyze each deal individually, and pursue the deals you are comfortable with. If you are very short of time but have money, pursue large deals. If you have time but not a lot of money, pursue smaller deals.

> A problem property can become a desirable one if the price is low enough. Just make sure to adjust the price you are willing to pay downward to reflect the challenges presented.

Section Five

Renovating and
Marketing Properties

11

Do Repairs Only—
Do Not Renovate!

So, you have made your great deal, and you have your new house. We will now discuss how the house should be prepared for market.

My theory of preparation is simple. The house should have all repairs completed, be spotlessly clean, freshly painted inside and out, curb appeal should be maximized, which means that the grass is cut, flower beds mulched, and all yard debris picked up. Do only the repairs necessary to make the house such that the new owner will not need to do any repairs when he moves into the property. Do not renovate or remodel the house and never "over-improve" a property by adding amenities that other houses in the neighborhood do not have, such as putting marble floors when all the other houses in the neighborhood have linoleum.

> Do only repairs necessary to make the house such that the new owner will not need to do any repairs when he moves into the property. Do not change floor plans and do additions.

Here are some ideas on how you can make your property sell quickly and for the best price. The idea is to make your house look TIDY, CLEAN, and WELL MAINTAINED.

How to Maximize Curb Appeal:

Curb appeal is the appearance of the house when someone pulls up by the curb in their car and takes their first look. It is crucial that your house look as attractive as possible. The good news is that there are inexpensive ways to make your house look great.

What You Should Do on the Outside of the House:
- Keep the lawn edged, cut and watered;
- Trim hedges, weed lawns and flowerbeds, and prune trees;
- Mulch the flower beds and under the shrubs;
- Add colorful plants and flowers near your front entrance and in front of the part of the house visible from the street;
- Put a wreath on the front door;
- Repair any cracked or crumbled areas of the foundation, steps, walkways, walls and patios;
- Power wash any wood, stucco or siding in need of cleaning;
- Clean and align gutters and down spouts;
- Repair any cracks and remove any weeds on the outside of the chimney;
- Replace loose or damaged roof shingles;
- Repair and repaint loose siding;
- Fill any gaps in siding or trim with caulk;
- Keep walks and driveways cleared of snow and ice;
- Fill in all potholes and cracks, re seal the driveway if it is asphalt;
- Keep your garage door closed;
- Remove all trash and debris. Store old and beaten up cars, motorcycles and boats off of the property;

- Clean the windows, siding and soffits. Bleach and power wash decks;
- Repaint the front door and trim around the door. Polish any brass and replace any worn out brass;
- Repaint any dull, chipped or peeling areas of the siding or trim, especially on the street side; use colors which are conservative and traditional for your area;
- Replace mailbox if worn out or old looking;
- Make sure the house has a visible number from the street so buyers can find it.

What You Should Do on the Inside of the House:
- Clean everything THOROUGHLY. Every room, closet, floor, window, drawer, basement, garage, storage area, etc.
- Get rid of any smells;
- Clear out all clutter, trash and debris;
- Repaint dingy, soiled or strongly colored walls attractive colors that match well. Look at sample homes for ideas or hire a decorator;
- Repair any broken items (glass, cabinets, toilets, sinks, etc.);
- Repair any water leaks from roofing or other water problems;
- Repair cracks, leaks, and signs of dampness in the attic and basement;
- Repair any and all water damage, cracks, holes or damage to plaster, wallboard, wallpaper, paint, and tiles;
- Replace broken or cracked windowpanes, moldings, and other woodwork.
- Repair the plumbing, heating, cooling, and alarm systems;
- Repair dripping faucets and showerheads;
- Buy showy new towels for the bathroom. Be sure to keep soap, toilet paper, a waste can and tissues available;
- In the kitchen install new cabinet knobs, new curtains, and a coat of paint. As with all paint, get dynamite colors that really "snap";
- Exterminate, if necessary;
- Have furniture for potential buyers to sit on, including a kitchen

table and a few chairs or have the home professionally staged;

- Keep some children's toys, coloring books, and crayons in the house to keep children occupied;
- Keep paper towels and cleaning materials handy. Have trash bags, a vacuum, dusting equipment, broom, and dustpan;
- Use bright light bulbs in all the rooms. Be sure to buy "soft white" bulbs. Avoid the "laundry room and basement bulbs" as they emit a poor quality of light;
- Consider having the home professionally "staged" with some furnishings.

You can help develop your eye for this by visiting model homes by builders in the area. They have professionals decorate their show homes. Look at the colors (inside and out), landscaping and brochures.

Average Return on Renovations			
Item	Approx. Retail Cost	Approx. Resale Value	Approx. Addtn'l Resale Value Per Dollar Spent
New Kitchen	$24,000	$16,000	$.60-.70
Add Bathroom	13,000	13,000	.70-.80
Remodel Bathroom	9,000	5,500	.60-.70
Add Family Room	35,000	22,000	.60-.70
Add Deck	6,000	3,000	.50-.70
Remodel Master Bdrm & Bath	25,000	15,000	.60-.70
Replace Windows	7,500	5,000	.60-.70
Add Attic Bdrm & Bath	24,000	18,000	.70-.80
New Siding	9,000	4,000	.50-.60

Comment: Remodeling projects lose money. This translates into an unnecessary loss in profits! Do not do projects which are not necessary to make the house saleable.

Other than work which must be done to make a house saleable (repairing broken items, cleaning, landscaping, painting as listed above), you should do very little. Remodeling, reconfiguration, or renovations are usually not financially beneficial to the renovator. The exhibit labeled "Average Return on Renovations" on the next page shows this very clearly. It is a chart showing the average return for various renovations based on my experience. The renovation work usually brings back less than 80% of the money put out to do the renovation!

Remember, typical buyers are busy people who will buy your house because it looks attractive, well maintained, and does not need any repairs for them to move in.

When considering which improvements or replacements to do, try to make your property similar to the average property in the neighborhood. If the other houses in the neighborhood have Formica™ counter-tops, yours should too do not put in Corian™ or granite counter-tops. You should not exceed the average because you will not get any additional money for your property even though you spent more. People generally identify a neighborhood they want to live in and then pick a house they can afford in that neighborhood. They usually stretch their budgets to get into the neighborhood. and do not have the money to pay extra for luxuries like whirlpool baths, solid brass fixtures, built-in appliances, or Corian™ counter-tops. Although buyers would like those features in a house, they are not able or willing to pay any extra money for them. You are in this for a profit, and you should not put extra money out for any amenities, repairs or improvements which do not provide you with a higher selling price in excess of their cost, or which are not absolutely necessary in order to make the property saleable.

Preparation You Should Not Do:
• Add rooms, decks or garages;
• Remodel bathroom, kitchen or other areas;
• Replace windows, unless the windows are broken; or
• Over-improvements with amenities not found in other homes
  in the neighborhood.

Speed is Important: Focus on getting the repairs and preparation done quickly. Every day that you own the house, it is costing you money in taxes, insurance, and lost opportunities because your money is invested and you may not be able to take advantage of another deal. As soon as you get the house, get started immediately clearing away debris, planning your renovations, and getting estimates. Focus on finishing the renovation quickly so that you can sell or rent the property, realize your profit, and get on to the next property.

Hire contractors to do the work. Your time is best used finding great deals, not swinging a hammer. If you do all of the work yourself, the renovations will take a long time. The carrying costs and lost opportunity costs from the delay will cost you as much as hiring a contractor would have cost.

Summary:
• Get the work done quickly.
• Maximize "curb appeal."
• Do all needed repairs.
• Do not add amenities not usually found in the neighborhood; and
• Make the house spotlessly clean.

12

Six Steps to Selling
Your Property Quickly

Why Speed is So Important: Holding Costs
and Opportunity Costs

Holding Costs: Each month you hold onto a property you incur holding costs. Holding costs are expenses such as taxes, insurance, and utility bills. Holding costs are profits flying out of your wallet. The quicker you turn a property around the less the holding costs accumulate and eat away at your profits. My flipper spreadsheet included in my Investor's Essentials form set calculates your monthly holding cost for you. Check our website at www.bobdiamondrealestate.com or call 800-608-0514 for more information.

Opportunity Costs: In addition to holding costs, there is also a hidden cost to holding property, called "opportunity costs." Opportunity costs are your costs for the profit you did not make on houses that you could not buy because your money was invested in the house that you already have. This is a fancy way of saying that if you are tied up in one deal, it will prevent you from doing other deals.

Six Steps to a Quick Sale
Step 1 - Repair - Do not Renovate!
Step 2 - Price the House Correctly
Step 3 - Stock and Prepare the House
Step 4 - Prepare Your Flyers and Brochures
Step 5 - Put a "For Sale" Sign Up
Step 6 - Follow-Up, Follow-Up, Follow-Up!

It is to your advantage to sell the property that you do have as quickly as possible. Let us consider methods that you can use to move your property quickly.

Step 1 - Repair only DO NOT RENOVATE

You will end up with a house that has all repairs completed, is freshly painted, attractively landscaped, and spotlessly clean. If you make the mistake of renovating, you will have spent too much on the property and will not be able to sell the property for enough money to make the profit you expected.

Step 2 - Price the House Correctly:

Re-do a comparable sales analysis. Supplement the analysis with a "competitive market analysis" by touring the other similar houses for sale in the area. Your buyers will probably look at all of the houses in their price range which are available in the area. Know the other houses competing with yours so you will be able to price your home to be competitive and you will be able to intelligently tell prospective buyers why your house is superior (i.e., cheaper, more rooms, better maintained, etc.). Price your house no more than 6% above what you perceive to be its fair market value based on your analysis. Do not price your house significantly above competing houses for sale.

Competitive Market Analysis: The Competitive Market Analysis method involves looking at competing houses for sale in the neighborhood. If I used it to estimate the proper listing price for the house at 2739 North 47th Street, the numbers would look like this:

Active Listings (houses for sale but not yet sold)			
Address	Asking Price	Days on Market	Notes
2713 N. 46th St.	$65,000	75	Same House, Better Street
2756 N. 46th St.	$65,500	102	Same House, Better Street
2733 N. 45th St.	$69,900	75	Same House, Quiet Street
4412 Sherwood Rd.	$69,900	78	Same House, Better Yard, Nicer street
Average =	$67,575	65	

Comment: The average asking price is $66,800 if we remove 4412 Sherwood from the analysis because it is on a better street with a better yard. I would price the home at $64,900.

If you are selling as a "for sale by owner" be aware that most buyers will want you to sell them the house less expensively because you do not have to pay a real estate agent. You will probably not make any extra money by selling by owner. You will probably have to give away most of the commission you would have paid to the real estate agent to the buyer as a discount or the property will not sell.

Step 3 - Stock and Prepare the House:

Have clean, attractive towels in the bathroom, toilet paper on the rolls, a coffee pot, a table and at least three chairs. Have some coloring books and children's toys in the kitchen in a box in the corner. The toys are in the house to entertain children while you discuss the house with any parents who come to see it. I often hire a professional "stager" to come into my houses to set up furniture and make the place shine like a dream house.

Step 4 - Prepare Your Flyers and Brochures:

Draw up flyers and brochures on the house and set them out on a table or counter top. The flyers will describe your property and give information about financing. Get some sample flyers from local houses for sale. Some of the best ones are done by regional and national builders. Provide at least the minimum amount of cash the buyer will need to bring to settlement, as well as the monthly payments the buyers should expect to pay if they have spotless credit, a 5, 10, and 20% down-payment, and sufficient income to obtain a fixed rate thirty year mortgage.

Include a Color Photograph of the House on the Flyer: Be sure your flyer includes a color photograph of the house.

Step 5 - Put a "For Sale" Sign on the Property:

It is very important that you have a visible sign on the property if you are "selling by owner". You should be able to purchase a sign for around $100.00.

> ### Use Photo Flyers
> I am a big fan of flyers with photographs. This helps prospective buyers remember your house. This "photo flyer" is a great marketing tool and very inexpensive.

Use a Box to hold Flyers This is a waterproof box similar to a mail box that mounts outside on the signpost and allows people driving by your property to help themselves to a flyer. The boxes are very effective because the prospect has your phone number in a convenient place and will remember what the phone number is because it is with the picture of the property. This is an inexpensive and effective marketing tool. The prospect has also already seen the property and likes the neighborhood and property. They are therefore a "warm" prospect. I believe they are marketed under the name Brochure Boxes.™ They also sell a tube-version at Home Depot.™

Step 6 - Follow-Up, Follow-Up, Follow-Up!

Follow-up is a habit of successful people. Adopt this habit. Follow-up with contractors, sign-makers, and flyer producers so your property is ready to sell as soon as possible. When a buyer comes

> **Buyers Lack Imagination**
> I have found that buyers cannot imagine what a property will look like when it is completed. Do not hold any open houses until the property is completely repaired, cleaned and staged

through your property, follow-up within a day or two to see if they are interested in purchasing the house. Once the house is under contract, follow-up to ensure that all the details are taken care of so the sale concludes as soon as possible.

Advertise Heavily: Do not cut corners in promoting your property. Advertise heavily. Run large photo ads in the local paper and hold open houses on weekends and week nights. Remember that you want to get this house sold as soon as possible and go on to the next deal. With heavy promotion, you will sell the house more quickly.

Dealing with Brokers: If a broker calls and says that he has a prospect, invite him to show the

> **Sample Newspaper Ad:**
> Oakville, 123 Main Street, Like New Single Family Home. Immaculate. 4BR, 1 2 baths. Huge living/dining room. Large Fenced in yard. New W/W Carpet, Paint, Roof. FOR SALE BY OWNER. This one won't last! $129,900. Call Sam 555-1212.

house and agree to pay him a commission if he makes the sale. In my area, this commission is generally about 3%, or half the full commission, which is usually 6% of the gross selling price. Unfortunately, many of the broker calls will be solicitations for listings. Tell the brokers up front if you have no interest in listing the property and that they should not come without their buyer.

Home Warranties: Another way to help sell your property is to offer a home warranty. A home warranty guarantees certain items will work for some time period after the sale, usually a year. The items that are guaranteed are usually the major items - heating, air conditioning, electrical, plumbing, and roofing systems. A typical cost would be in the neighborhood of $400.00 for a home warranty.

Home warranties can be good marketing tools, because they generally cost little and provide some peace of mind to the buyer.

You will not generally obtain a higher price for a home with a home warranty, but a home warranty can help to overcome an objection of a nervous buyer. If you want to offer a home warranty, you can check with your real estate agent on where to get one and some of the warranty companies. One company is First American Financial, which has a web-site named "HTTP://WWW. FIRSTAM.COM."

Do Not Discriminate for Illegal Reasons! Under the fair housing laws, which are Federal and apply in all fifty states, it is illegal to discriminate against people in the sale or rental of housing for many reasons. Examples include because of the tenants' or buyers' race, religion, marital status, age (unless they are under the age when they can legally enter into a contract), sexual preference, disability, religion, family status or because they have or don't have children.

This is federal law and applies as a MINIMUM in all states. Your individual State may have more strict rules for you to follow. You are, however, subject to the federal rules in addition to the state rules.

There are actually agencies that send out "testers" to try to rent or buy housing to see if they are discriminated against. If they find discrimination, they sue!

In any ads that you place, you should not refer to these factors. Do not ask prospective buyers about this information. Do not suggest the house is not good for the buyers because of their race, family size or because of any of the above factors. Do not refer to a house based on its proximity to any known religious or racial landmarks - IE; "it is close to the synagogues."

You can and should discriminate against buyers if they are not financially qualified to borrow money to buy the house because of insufficient income, savings, or credit!

13

Should You Hire a Real Estate Agent to Market Your Property?

Consider Hiring an Agent to Place the Property on the MLS Only

If you are experienced in real estate, consider hiring an agent who, for a fee up front, will put your property on the MLS system. Sign a written agreement with them that if they find a prospect and put together the sale, you will give them a commission, but, if you find a prospect and sell the house to that prospect, there will be no commission. Most agents do not like this kind of arrangement, but, if you shop around, you should be able to find someone who will place your house on the MLS for a flat fee.

Use Ninety-Day Listing Agreements:

If you do hire a real estate agent to market your property, you should hire them in ninety day increments. Prior to hiring the agent, you should also insist that the agent tell you how many open houses will be held, how much advertising will be done, and the marketing plan for the property.

Keep the Foreclosure News to Yourself.

Do not volunteer to the real estate agent or anyone else connected with marketing the property that the property was a foreclosure.

If a buyer knows that it is a foreclosure, they will immediately want a great deal and will make only low offers. If you tell the real estate agent, he may tell prospective customers.

If you are asked about the foreclosure, do not lie. Laws have been changing over the past ten years or so. The new laws require sellers to disclose their knowledge about a property. Do not hide information from buyers. It is unfair, unethical, and can get you in legal trouble.

Consult with your local attorney or real estate agent about disclosure laws in your state and follow them.

Some agents work very hard by creating web-sites, attractive brochures, and heavily advertising the property. Others do very little other than listing the house on the market. If the agent does not want to provide this information or is not going to do much, you should probably use a different agent.

Whether you hire an agent to market your property or not, you must get your property known to prospective buyers. Tell the neighbors about the house, ask them if they know anyone looking to move into the neighborhood. Put ads anywhere people from the community congregate, such as on bulletin boards of local hospitals, churches and synagogues.

If you are selling a more expensive house, one above $300,000, you must get it on the MLS system. The buyers in the higher price ranges are not as likely to look for "For Sale by Owner" houses. They instead hire a real estate agent and look at the properties the Agent takes from the MLS computer. The agents usually do not want to bother looking for "For Sale by Owner" property and will not show your property unless the buyers specifically ask to see it.

If you do hire an agent, use one who works FULL TIME in real estate and who makes their living at it. The "Part Timers" and people who just use it as a supplemental income will not usually work as hard to sell the property. This is because a hobbyist is not as motivated as someone who is depending upon the sale of property to provide their next meal!

A real estate agent will simplify your transaction because they handle the showings, qualifying the buyers, placing ads, drafting the contract for sale, and taking telephone calls. They also do the work necessary to get the property to settlement which involves many, many details. The real estate agent will cost you money, usually 6% of the selling price. Whether an agent is the right choice for you depends upon your individual situation and you should do what you are most comfortable with.

14

Tips On Dealing
With Buyers

Understand How Your Buyer is Feeling

People get nervous about buying a house. A house is the largest single purchase most people make in their lives. They have heard horror stories of termites, floods, deals gone bad, and money lost. First time home buyers are even more nervous.

Deal gently with buyers. Address the concerns which underlie their nervousness. Find out what they are looking for in a house and fit your sales presentation into those concerns.

If they want a three bedroom home in like-new condition, in the same school system as yours, remind them the house is in the school system they want, has the size they need, and has just been renovated. You motivate the buyers to act by having an appealing house in good condition.

Find out your buyer's concerns and worries and address them directly. If they are nervous about underlying problems with the house, tell them they will have the opportunity to have a home inspector or contractor inspect the house for them to check for problems. The inspection will include the roof, plumbing, heating, cooling, and electrical systems, as well as the structure of the house. Any problems will be spotted and addressed.

If they are nervous about how the papers will be put together, tell them you will have your attorney or real estate agent prepare them and go over the papers with them. Assure them they can have their own attorney or real estate agent review the papers before they are committed.

If the buyers are unsure about where to turn for a mortgage, have a few lender phone numbers handy.

Dealing With First-Time Buyers Special Challenge - Lack of Savings:

The problem for most first time buyers is that they lack the money to make closing. This means they do not have enough savings to make the down payment required by the mortgage company, plus pay the closing costs such as pre-paid taxes, insurance, title insurance, etc. necessary to buy the property. If, however, the buyers are able to gather the initial money needed to purchase the house, they are able to make the monthly payment.

There are two easy techniques you can use to meet the first time buyers' needs and make a sale quickly at full market price. Those techniques are the Seller Assist and Lease-Option.

Seller Assist: This means the seller will give the buyer money to help them pay the down payment and closing costs they need to purchase the house. The great thing to this technique is that you can do a "seller assist" of several thousand dollars without it costing you much!

This is how a seller assist works: the seller agrees to sell the house to the buyer for a higher price than the seller is actually willing to sell the property; the extra money is then given back to the buyer at the settlement table; and he uses that money to pay his closing costs and down-payment!

This is perfectly legal so long as the mortgage company is aware of the "Seller Assist." The mortgage companies will generally allow about 3% of the purchase price to be used towards a "Seller Assist."

The exact steps to follow are the following:
- Determine for what amount the seller would be willing to sell the property. Let's assume that figure was $100,000;
- Next, add on 3% of that figure. The selling price in our example would be $103,000;
- Draw up the agreement of sale for $103,000 with a $3,000 credit from seller to buyer at settlement.

FROM SELLER'S PERSPECTIVE

Item	Without Seller Assist	With Seller Assist
Sale Price on Contract	$100,000	$103,000
3% Seller Assist		$(3,090)
Net Cash to Seller	$100,000	$99,910

FROM BUYERS' PERSPECTIVE

Item	Without Seller Assist	With Seller Assist
Sale Price on Contract	$100,000	$103,000
3% Seller Assist		$(3,090)
Mortgage (95% of Sale Price)	$(95,000)	$(97,850)
Settlement Costs & Fees	$3,940	$3,940
Cash Needed at Settlement	$8,940	$6,000

Comments: Everybody wins! This exhibit shows the effect on the buyer and seller due to the "seller assist". The net effect upon the buyer is that he needs much less money to make settlement.

The result is that the seller will then receive the $100,000 he wants, and the buyer will need less cash at settlement. The buyer will need less cash because he is receiving $3,000 towards his closing costs from the seller.

This will not work if the house will not appraise for at least the total sale price, including the seller assist. The plan will not work if the appraisal is insufficient because the lender will lend the base its loan on LESSER of the Agreement of sale price or the amount of the Appraisal. This usually does not cause a problem.

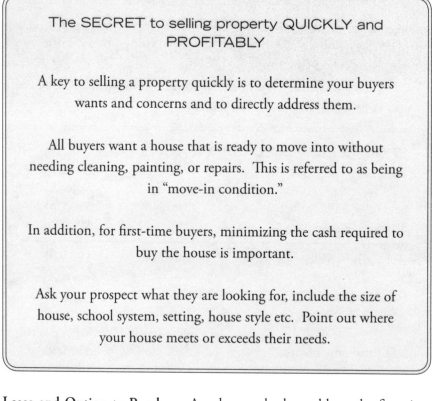

The SECRET to selling property QUICKLY and PROFITABLY

A key to selling a property quickly is to determine your buyers wants and concerns and to directly address them.

All buyers want a house that is ready to move into without needing cleaning, painting, or repairs. This is referred to as being in "move-in condition."

In addition, for first-time buyers, minimizing the cash required to buy the house is important.

Ask your prospect what they are looking for, include the size of house, school system, setting, house style etc. Point out where your house meets or exceeds their needs.

Lease and Option to Purchase: Another method to address the first time buyer's lack of money to make settlement is to offer a lease with option to purchase. This is when a buyer rents (leases) the property for a set time period and has an option to purchase it by or before the end of a lease period at an agreed-upon price.

The buyer puts down a non-refundable up-front deposit and pays extra rent every month If the buyer exercises his option, the extra rent is credited towards the buyer's down payment and closing costs. Additionally, the security deposit, last month's rent and option fee that the buyer paid at the beginning of the lease purchase will be credited towards his purchase, which means that the buyer may be able to come to settlement with no additional cash.

Typically, the buyer must perform all the repairs on the property during the lease period which means the seller will have no repair costs. The tenants are easy to manage because they plan on buying the property and will take care of it.

The disadvantage of a "lease with option to purchase" is the time you must wait between the time the buyer leases and when he finally purchases. This can tie up your money. Another disadvantage is that the buyer may never buy the house. If the house is in a rapidly declining area, this is a problem. Your protection from problems is the up-front option money and additional rent and option fee you collect each month. Even if the buyer never buys, you will make more money than if you did not enter into a lease-option.

Some people use a lease-purchase agreement which obligates the buyer to buy the property. I do not use those agreements because you can create a title problem by giving the tenant rights in the property. If you are in Texas, you need to be especially careful because those transactions are regulated.

I calculate the actual terms by working backwards. I determine what the buyer would need to pay to purchase the property, including down payment and all settlement costs. I then demand about 1/5 to 1/3 of that amount for the initial "option fee." I divide the balance left over a one to three year time period (depending upon my needs and the buyer's financial abilities), with even payments each month.

Benefits of a Lease-Option: The benefits of a lease-option to you as the seller is that you can get the property to quickly produce income and you have almost no rental headaches. Your headaches will be minimal because

Lease-Option Example
From Buyer's Perspective

Item	Amount	Comments
Up-Front Option Fee	$1,500	Non-refundable - credited to buyer if he buys
Monthly Option Fee	$100	Non-refundable - credited to buyer f he buys
Monthly Rent	$650	Rent is same as non-lease option deal
Settlement Costs to Buyer	$5,600	

Credits at Settlement

Up-Front and Monthly Option Fees	$5,100	Up-front fee plus monthly Option Fees
Security Deposit	$650	
Total Credit Available Towards Settlement	$5,750	

From Seller's Perspective

Item	Amount	Comments
Up-Front Option Fee	$1,500	Non-refundable - credited to buyer if he buys
Total Monthly Option Fees Collected	$3,600	Non-refundable - credited to buyer if he buys
Total Additional profit to Seller if Buyer does not go through with the purchase	$5,100	If Buyer does not make settlement, (very common) seller makes out! Seller Keeps Up-Front Option fee and $100 per month option fees

the tenant is responsible for maintaining the property. Since the tenant has so much money invested in the property, he usually will not default on the lease. Tenants who default on the lease lose their right to purchase the property, as well as all of the deposit and rent credit they have built up. You then end up keeping the option fee and option payments the tenant paid over the term of the option.

When to Use the Lease-Option: A lease-option is typically used to help sell to a first-time buyer who lacks the cash necessary to make settlement or who needs time to resolve credit problems before he can get a mortgage.

A sample of a Lease-Option Agreement is included in with the forms. Consult your attorney before signing anything. These documents should be used only with the advice and counsel of a competent attorney and accountant who are looking at your individual situation. You should not use these forms without that advice and counsel.

Explanation (Table on opposite Page): Lets say I have a house that I want to sell for $60,000. The rent on similar houses is $650 per month. A buyer needs $5,600 to pay the closing costs and down-payment necessary to purchase the house. If he purchases, he will have a payment of $600 per month, including taxes and insurance. If the person were to rent, his move-in expenses would probably be three month's rent (first month's rent, security deposit of one month and last month's rent) which is $1,950.

I would propose the following lease-option terms: $1,500 up front fee (non-refundable) for the option to purchase, plus a monthly option fee of $100 per month for 36 months in addition to the regular rent. The up-front fee and monthly option fee are credited towards the purchase price if he buys the property. If the buyer does not buy the property, the landlord (you) keeps the money. The tenant pays all utilities and repairs during the lease option period and has two years to complete the purchase.

At the end of a three-year period, the buyer would have a total credit of $5,750 from the up-front fee, monthly option fee and security deposit back at settlement. The buyer could make settlement without bringing any additional cash. If the buyer never settles, at the end of three years you will have $5,100 more money than you would have otherwise had ($1,500 up-front fee and $3,600 in monthly option fees).

15

Showing the House

Collect Information About Prospective Buyers

When a prospective buyer comes to your open house, greet them, introduce yourself, have them fill in a paper with their name, phone number, and address. If they are represented by a broker, get that person's name, address, and phone number. Note how they found out about the house so that you will know which marketing technique is working for you.

The Tour Next give the prospective buyers a tour of the house. As you are showing the buyers around, point out any new items in the house such as water heater, roof, etc. Highlight the good aspects of the house including the design, neighborhood, convenience, etc. Answer the buyer's questions. Ask the buyers when they want to move and what they want in a house.

After you have shown people through your house, if the house is vacant, invite them to walk around by themselves and give them a chance to talk among themselves about the house. (If the house is occupied or has belongings in it, keep the buyers with you so there is no theft.) If the buyers are still interested when they return from their tour, they will want to talk to you about the specifics of purchasing the house. You should then offer the photo flyers and go through the information on the price, potential loans available, and warranties on any new items (i.e., roof, heater) in the house, etc.

If the Buyers are Interested in Pursuing a Sale: Ask them if they are pre-qualified for a loan or have cash to buy the house. If they are pre-qualified, ask to see their pre-qualification letter. (Pre-qualification letter is a letter from a mortgage company stating how much money the buyer is qualified to borrow). If the prospective buyer needs a mortgage and has not been pre-qualified, have them fill in the buyer's information sheet so you will have the information necessary to evaluate their ability to qualify for a mortgage. (Sample copy immediately follows and can also be found in the forms set.)

Evaluate the Buyers Ability to Buy Before Committing Yourself: The buyer's ability to buy must be evaluated and confirmed BEFORE entering into an Agreement of Sale because once the Agreement of Sale is signed, you are obligated to abide by its terms. The terms typically allow from thirty to ninety days for the buyer to obtain a mortgage. If the buyer is turned down for the mortgage, he gets his deposit back and does not have to purchase the house.

You effectively cannot market the property once you enter into an Agreement of Sale, so you can waste up to ninety days while the buyer is trying to obtain a mortgage. On top of the wasted time, you could miss the best selling season (generally March through June), and have to pay the holding costs while waiting for the buyer to get a mortgage.

Unless the buyers are pre-qualified by a mortgage company and can show you a letter to that effect, have the prospective buyers fill in a Buyer's Financial Form and give it to you. Have a real estate agent or mortgage lender help

> ## Is the person standing before you a 'Prospect' or a "suspect"?
>
> Many people claiming to be real estate buyers will waste your time without mercy. It may be lack of knowledge, it may be lack of respect. But in any event it is a waste of your time.
>
> The person touring your house is a "prospect" if he wants to buy a house NOW, has cash to buy the house or sufficiently good credit, savings, and income to qualify for a mortgage.
>
> Prospective buyers often do not know if they will qualify for a mortgage to buy the house. Screening prospective buyers for their ability to buy is one of the services your real estate agent performs. If you are going without an agent, you must sort out early on whether the person touring the house is able to buy. This must be accomplished BEFORE you sign an Agreement of Sale with the buyer.
>
> Screen the prospects by having them fill out the "buyers information" form. Pull the person's credit and then review the information with a lender.

you evaluate their ability to buy. Pull a credit report on the buyer and evaluate his credit.

Be Firm on the Financial Information: Americans are very private about their financial information. You need to know about the prospective buyers credit, income, and savings so you can evaluate whether they will be able to borrow money to buy your house. If the buyer does not need a mortgage, you just need the information necessary to confirm they have the money to pay for the house and closing costs. Many buyers will resist giving you their financial information. Tell a buyer who resists giving you their financial information that unless they meet with a lender and obtain a pre-approval letter, you will only enter into an agreement of sale with them if they will put a 10% deposit down on the house and will accept an Agreement of Sale without a mortgage contingency. This means that if they are not approved for a mortgage, they will still have to buy the house or will lose their deposit.

The following form called a "Buyer Information Form" will help you to gather the financial information you will from the buyer. You can then order a credit report and run the buyers finances through the computerized mortgage qualification form included with the forms set. You can also get help determining if buyers will qualify for a mortgage from a real estate agent or mortgage broker. Many web-sites have mortgage pre-qualification sheets as well. I have included a list of some of those web-sites in my Internet Directory.

Money Saving Tip

You can save money by reaching a business agreement with the owner or prospective buyer BEFORE you hire a professional to draft the contract.

Write down an outline of your agreement with the owner in the form of "Letter of Intent" that I have on included on the forms CD-ROM. Both the buyer and seller sign the "Letter of Intent" and then take it to an attorney to translate into a binding contract.

Banks generally use a consistent set of guidelines to determine the amount of loan an applicant qualifies for:

- The prospective borrowers total monthly debt expenses, including the proposed mortgage payment, should not exceed 36% of the borrower's total monthly income.

- The total monthly mortgage payment should not exceed 28% of the prospective borrower's income without considering monthly debt.

Buyer Information Form

BUYERS WHO NEED A MORTGAGE TO BUY THE PROPERTY MUST INCLUDE ALL FINANCIAL INFORMATION, CASH BUYERS NEED ONLY SHOW THE FUNDS NECESSARY TO PURCHASE THE PROPERTY

	Buyer 1	Buyer 2
Name:		
Address:		
Phone #		
SSN:		
Employer:		
Employer Address:		
# Of Years:		
Occupation:		
Post Tax Monthly Salary:		
Overtime:		
Previous Employment:		
# Of Years:		
Occupation:		
Reason For Leaving:		

How Much Money Do You Plan To Borrow To Buy The Property?

_____

What Is The Source Of Your Deposit On The Property?

_____

What Is Your Source Of Funds For Settlement Charges?

_____

Liquid Assets:

Bank Or Investment Accounts (Name)	Type Of Account	Balance or Value
_____	_____	_____
_____	_____	_____
_____	_____	_____

U.s. Savings Bonds (Current Value)	_____	_____
Stock Certificates (Current Value)	_____	_____
Cash Surrender Value Of Insurance:	_____	_____
Profit Sharing (Vested Interest)	_____	_____
Other:	_____	_____

Liabilities:

Creditor Name	Min. Monthly Payment	Balance Due	Number Of Months Left To Pay
Auto: _____			
Auto: _____			
Furniture: _____			

Installment: _____

Student Loans: _____

Charge Card: _____

Charge Card: _____

Charge Card: _____

Other: _____

Total Debts: _____

Have You Filed Bankruptcy?

Yes _____ No _____ Year Discharged _____

Year Filed _____ Type (Chapter 7, 13 Etc.): _____

Disposable Income: Buyer One   Buyer Two

Net Monthly Income After Taxes _____ _____

Net Monthly Income After Taxes _____ _____

Other Income: _____ _____

Total Net Monthly Income: _____ _____

Less Total Monthly Payments: (_____)(_____)

Disposable Income: _____ _____

By signing below I (We) hereby certify that the foregoing information is true and accurate to the best of my knowledge and belief. I (We) understand that the above information will be revealed to the owner of the property that I (We) have submitted an offer on. This information is not for loan purposes but is for the purpose of the owner of the property evaluating my ability to borrow money to purchase the property. I understand and agree that the property owner or his agent may run a credit report(s) to ascertain my ability to obtain a mortgage and investigate to verify information on this form.

Buyer One:_____ Date:_____

Buyer Two:_____ Date:_____

Buyer Qualification Example

Buyer Mortgage Qualification Spreadsheet
(A WORKING ELECTRONIC VERSION is in the forms set)

Buyer's Name: Wanda Buyer
Property: 123 Main Street,
Anytown, USA

Monthly Non-Housing Debt Payments		Monthly Income	
Credit Cards:	$175	Monthly Salary before Taxes:	$7,000.00
Car Payment;	$350	Monthly Interest Income:	$100
Other Loan Payments		Other Monthly Income	
Monthly Non-Housing Debt:	$525	Total Monthly Income:	$7,100

Debt-to-Income Calculations		Mortgage Buyer Can Afford	
Current Debt-to-Income:	7.39%	Term of Loan (Years);	30
Total % Allowed:	36.00%	Annual Interest Rate %:	8%
Available % for Payment*:	28.00%	Payment:	$1,988
Maximum Payment:	$1,988	Maximum Loan:	$270,932

Price of The House		Mortgage The Buyer	
Buyer Can Afford		Plans on Applying For	
Cash Available	$12,000	Term of Loan (Years)	30
Closing Costs,			
Estimated	$2,829	Annual Interest Rate %	8.00%
Required Cash			
Reserve	$3,976	Loan Amount	$100,000.00
Remaining Cash			
for Down	$5,194	Calculated Payment	$733.76
Maximum Price			
of House	$276,126	Short/Over	$1,254.24

Note: If the buyer is "Short" (meaning the above Short/over figure is negative), then the buyer cannot qualify for a loan under normal lending practices.

The spreadsheet I included on the diskette automatically performs these calculations.

Some loan programs, such as the FHA, HUD, and other programs can allow prospective borrowers to borrow more money to buy a house and therefore spend a higher percentage of their income on housing. Check with a lender in your area to see what is available.

In addition to monthly debt payment to income ratios, there are a number of other factors that can influence the bank's decision to grant a mortgage loan:

- The "L.T.V." or "Loan to Value." This is the amount of money the lender is lending compared to the value of the property. For example, if a bank was lending $80,000 against a house worth $100,000, the "L.T.V." would be 80%. The banks are more comfortable lending lower "L.T.V." because the collateral they are lending against is worth proportionally more than the money they are lending. If the borrower defaults and they have to foreclose, the chance of the bank recovering all it is owed from the foreclosure sale is better.

• The amount of cash the buyer has leftover after he pays his down-payment and loan closing costs.

• How much money the prospective borrower had been spending on rent or previous mortgage.

• How much more money than average you make. Lenders sometimes assume that if you make a lot more money than average you can afford a higher percentage of your income on a mortgage payment.

Follow-up is Important:

The buyers will probably want to go home to think about whether to purchase the house. Tell them that you are actively marketing the property. If they are interested, they should act quickly. Most buyers are not ready to pursue the purchase of a house until they have a chance to think about it overnight. They will usually call to see the house a second time if they have an interest.

Do not unduly pressure buyers. Use mild pressure only. The purchase of a house is a big decision and buyers are nervous. If they feel too much pressure it will make them uncomfortable with you. They will then be less likely to buy from you. The pressure you should apply is to let them know you are showing the house to more people. Try to create the impression that if they do not act, the opportunity will get away. Play up the features and benefits of the house and comment that it will sell soon if they do not buy it.

Follow-up with all people who came to see the house twenty-four hours after you first met them. Ask the buyers if they want to make an offer on the house. If they are not interested, ask them why. This is cheap research and will inform you of any weak areas of your house.

16

Agreements of Sale

What is an Agreement of Sale?

An Agreement of Sale is a contract between a buyer and seller. It calls for the seller to sell and the buyer to buy a piece of real estate within a certain time, for a certain price. Contracts to buy and sell real estate must be in writing or the contract cannot be enforced. You MUST get the agreement in writing! Next give the prospective buyers a tour of the house. As you are showing the buyers around, point out any new items in the house such as water heater, roof, etc. Highlight the good aspects of the house including the design, neighborhood, convenience, etc. Answer the buyer's questions. Ask the buyers when they want to move and what they want in a house.

At a minimum, the contract must specify the buyer and seller, price, real estate being sold, and settlement date. The contract should specify much more. Items which should be included are whether the sale is contingent upon buyer obtaining a mortgage,

> **Tip**
> If you do not want to spend the money on a professional to prepare the Agreement of Sale, you are inviting trouble. Get professional help with the Agreement of Sale until you have experience in the business. Attorneys are usually the appropriate professionals.

what happens if there is a title problem, whether a home inspection will be performed, and more. A sample Agreement of Sale is included in the forms set. There is one for the buyer and another for the seller. Be sure to have a local attorney review the form agreement of sale before you use it. If the seller is in default on their real estate taxes or a loan there are even more

> **Contingencies**
> Contingencies are events or circumstances which can let a buyer or seller out of an agreement of sale. An example is a mortgage contingency.
>
> If an agreement of sale has a mortgage contingency as a part of the Agreement, it means the buyer is only required to buy the property if he obtains a mortgage. If he is rejected for a mortgage, then he is not required to buy the house and will be given his deposit back.
>
> Generally speaking, buyers want a lot of contingencies which allow them to get out of an Agreement of Sale if they change their mind, are unable to obtain financing, or if the house is not in the mechanical condition they hoped for.
>
> Sellers want few contingencies so they are more certain an Agreement of Sale will go through and the house will sell.

requirements in other states including Illinois, Minnesota and California. I have specialized forms available for use in those states.

If You Are a Novice, Hire a Professional

If you are new to real estate, you should have your real estate broker or attorney handle the agreement of sale and settlement. Entering into a bad Agreement of Sale can be a nightmare and can easily lead to lawsuits.

Real Estate Sales Are Relatively Complicated: There are many details which need to be attended to, and an attorney or real estate broker will make certain they are addressed. The details can include obtaining Certificates of Occupancy, scheduling settlement, hiring a title company, researching title, straightening out title issues, making sure the buyer has his inspections and applications done in a timely manner, etc. Until you are experienced, use someone with experience to attend to these details. I have a closing checklist on the forms set to help you keep track of the details once you take over the transactions.

Use an Attorney If You Already Have a Buyer: I have found that if you already have a buyer, it is usually less expensive to use an attorney to draw up the contracts and handle the details necessary to complete the sale. This presumes you are using an attorney who focuses on real estate. Do not use an attorney who does not focus on real estate or you will tend to have problems rather than help getting your sale consummated.

A Note About Escrow Accounts

The buyers deposit should stay in a separate account. This is called an "escrow" account. It is controlled by a third party such as a real estate broker, title company, or attorney. If you are buying a house, you should never give the deposit directly to the seller. Should the deal fall apart, you might have trouble getting your deposit back because the seller might have spent the money. If you are selling a house, you should either keep the money in a separate savings account or let a title company or attorney hold it.

Section Six

Making It All Work

17

Your Winning Team

To succeed at this business, you will need a team of professionals to assist you. Your team will consist of contractors, title searchers, lenders, attorneys, accountants, bankers, and an appraiser. You do not need to find all of these people right now. You will need some of them at various times to assist you. Let us consider each of their roles.

Contractors

Your contractor will help you in two ways: First in evaluating a potential property for the cost of renovation, then once you get the property to quickly renovate it. You should choose a contractor based on recommendations from others you trust.

Once you have selected your contractor, you must manage him properly. This means two things. First, you will enter into a written contract with your contractor which states the work which is to be done with specific time frames, second you adhere to the "Golden Rule" so that you stay in control of the project.

Be Firm, Fair and Demanding: Deal with the contractors the same way you would deal with anyone else in business; be firm, be fair, live up to your part of the agreement, and insist that others live up to their promises also. Do not be indecisive. Keep it clear that you expect the contractor to perform on time and on budget. If the contractor does not show up, call him immediately and do not allow him to abandon your project.

Appraisers

The appraiser is an expert in estimating the value of properties. You can use an appraiser to help you determine the value of a property whose value you cannot pinpoint.

You will not use the appraiser very frequently unless you are using him to supply you with comparables. You can wait to add this member to your team when you actually need him.

> ### Appraiser Designations
> All appraisers do not have the same experience and training. There are many designations earned by appraisers depending upon their area of concentration and training. Try to use appraisers with training and experience which matches your project. The professional designations of the appraiser can help you to know if the appraiser is a good match for your project. These designations are from the Appraisal Institute which is an international association of more than 20,000 real estate professionals. The Institute offers general and residential designations to qualified members. Here are some of the designations:

MAI designation is held by appraisers who are experienced in the valuation and evaluation of commercial, industrial, residential, and other types of properties, and who advise clients on real estate investment decisions.

SRPA designation is held by appraisers who are experienced in the valuation of commercial, industrial, residential, and other types of property.

SREA designation is held by appraisers who are experienced in real estate valuation and analysis and advise clients on real estate investment decisions.

SRA designation is held by appraisers who are experienced in the valuation of single-family homes, townhouses, and residential income properties of up to and including four units.

RM designation is held by appraisers who are experienced in the valuation of single-family dwellings and two-, three-, and four-unit residential properties.

MAI is a general appraiser, certified to appraise any property from residences to industrial property or even timberland. An SRA is a residential appraiser, certified to appraise dwellings, including single family homes, apartments, condominiums, retirement homes, etc."

My Internet Directory has web-sites to help you find an appraiser.

Attorneys:

You must have a competent real estate attorney to advise you. He must be familiar with foreclosure, zoning, landlord tenant law, and all litigation which can arise around real estate. Since you are a small investor, it will probably be more appropriate for you to work with a solo practitioner or a small law firm of from one to three attorneys.

An attorney who specializes in real estate and foreclosures will have the experience needed to give you the best advice. He should be able to quickly and efficiently perform evictions, ejectments, title transfers, loan documentation, deeds, and agreements of sale.

He must be readily available for telephone consultations.

If you are having trouble finding an attorney, ask other investors and real estate agents. You can also consult a guide called Martindale-Hubbell™ which is available on the Internet (see my Internet Guide for the web-site address).

Call some of the recommended attorneys and discuss your business plans with them. When you find someone knowledgeable with whom you are comfortable, that is probably the right person for your team.

Title Companies:

It is critical that you have a good resource person to help you with title work. There are two types of professionals that can help you with title questions: title companies and attorneys. In some states, attorneys are responsible for checking and approving titles; in other states, there are title companies. You need to establish a good relationship with an attorney or title company whom you can call upon as a resource when needed.

A good place to start if you want to find a knowledgeable title company is to ask the party conducting the foreclosure sales to tell you who handles their title work. The sheriff, trustee, or other person conducting the sale usually needs title work to determine who should receive the proceeds from the foreclosure sale. You should also ask for referrals from other investors, attorneys, and real estate agents.

When you have these names, call them and check into the person's experience and attitude. The best fit for a small investor is probably going to be with a small title company. You need someone who is accessible and who will take the time to explain title issues to you.

The Golden Rule

Remember the Golden Rule He who has the gold makes the rules. Keep your gold so you make the rules. Do not give large deposits. If you have contractors who demand a deposit of more than 10% of the job cost, tell them that you do not do business that way, but that you will pay them regularly for the work that has been done, as it is completed.

If a contractor insists that he needs a deposit for materials, tell him that you will get the materials and bring them on site for him or will pay him for the materials once he brings them on site and shows paid receipts. Paid receipts are important because an unpaid supplier may be able to lien your property with a "materialmans lien or "mechanics lien if the supplier is not paid for the materials.

Why the "Golden Rule?"

If a contractor is pre paid, he will often start to do things such as not show up, doing other jobs while he is supposed to be doing your job, and will otherwise generally misbehave. This happens because he has the gold and is in control of your project.

In all construction contracts, you should have deadlines for completion of tasks and should work from a written contract. Specify in the contract when the work is to be completed, list the work to be done, the materials to be used, and the prices to be paid for each segment of work.

You will need the title company or attorney for three reasons:

- To provide quick-and-dirty searches, often called last owner searches. This refers to checking the public records to see what liens are recorded against the property indexed under the current owner's name. To do this, you will need a supplier who is fast and inexpensive. I usually pay up to $45 for this type of search; (Note: this search will not find liens against the property indexed against former owners! Do not invest your money until you get a more comprehensive search. Use it as a screening tool only)

- To tell you which liens will be divested in the event of a foreclosure sale;

- To issue you title insurance. The title issuer will take care of any title problems you have after purchasing the property and will protect you from losing the property or having to pay an unexpected bill due to a title problem. You should purchase title insurance whenever possible at the time you purchase a property.

Real Estate Agents:

You will use a real estate agent for several things, the first of which is to supply comparables when you are trying to determine the value of a property. A real estate agent can also market a property for you. The real estate agent may also occasionally have a good deal for you. Remember that real estate agents generally sell at retail, so they are not our primary source for properties.

You should find a real estate agent in the same way that you find any competent professional ask other investors, friends, family, and neighbors for referrals. Interview recommended agents. Always hire an agent who is actively selling houses in the neighborhood in which you are buying or selling.

Other Investors:

Develop relationships with other investors who are interested in different areas, or in different types of properties, than you are. Then, you can freely share information without compromising your business opportunities. I have my mastermind groups for just this purpose. Mastermind is available once you have completed one or more of my live seminar programs. Call my office at 800-608-0514 or go to my website www.bobdiamondrealestate.com for more information.

18

Financing Your
Real Estate Purchases

What's the matter, short of money? Not to worry. Almost every new investor comes into the business short of money, knowledge, or time. You are solving the knowledge deficiency by taking this course. If you have time, but limited money, you will simply need to cultivate some sources of funding. Some of these may be:

- partnering with someone who has money to invest or the ability to borrow;
- cash advances from credit cards;
- home equity lines of credit;
- self directed IRAs;
- mortgages; or
- friends, family, and investor clubs.

What you must balance is the cost of borrowing the money versus the potential profit in the deal. If the deal is lucrative, you can afford to pay a high interest rate so long as the terms of the loan are good. The terms you should try to negotiate are no payments until the house is sold and 100% financing of the purchase and fix up costs. You try to minimize the points up front. "Points" are fees paid to a lender. Each "point" is 1% of the loan amount. Points are paid at the time the loan is made.

The terms are important because the income from the sale of the property is matched to the expenses to purchase and renovate the property. During the time that the house is being renovated, it is not usually producing revenue. Any investor would be very unhappy every month in which he had to make payments on a property without receiving income from that property. Getting involved with too many payments going out, with no money coming in is a recipe for bankruptcy.

A lender should be comfortable with lending against the real estate because you are asking to borrow no more than 80% of the retail value of the property, including fix up costs. The lender is well-protected in case he has to foreclose due to the cushion of equity.

Let's take a look at each financing option and discuss the benefits and drawbacks of each.

Partnerships

One option you have is to enter into a partnership. In my experience, the partnership which works best is one in which both partners need each other because they are bringing different talents, abilities, or resources to the partnership. For example, if you are going to be the active partner who finds and negotiates the deal, and handles renovation and marketing, you will need a passive partner who prefers to sit in the background, put up the money, and let you and the money work for him. In that situation, active and passive partners generally split the profits 50/50.

If you are going to enter into a partnership, be sure to enter into a written partnership agreement, so that everyone is clear about his or her responsibilities. The documents control the relationship between your partner and yourself. They are very important and a competent attorney should draft a custom document for you. Tax implications may be very important and you must consult with an accountant prior to entering into the partnership. I have included a sample partnership form in the forms set to get you started.

Here is a list of things to discuss with your potential partner PRIOR to visiting your attorney and accountant so you can save money on professional fees. Discuss the following items and come to an agreement about them prior to seeking the help of an attorney and accountant:

- Initial monetary contributions of the partners.

- On-going monetary contributions of the partners. (Estimated needs and timing, who will put up the money and when.)

- Contribution by partners of their time and skills to the business of the partnership. Any compensation they expect to receive.

- Who will manage the renovations, pick contractors, and supervise them.

- Who will manage the properties if they are rented long-term.

- Who will manage the money.

- Whether the partners agree to do all deals together or reserve the right to do deals outside the partnership.

- Who can sign contracts and hire workers for the partnership.

- Who will get what percentage of the profits.

- Duration of the partnership.

Final Steps to Form the Partnership:

- Consult with accountant to discuss tax implications, possible methods to distribute tax benefits, other alternative forms of business (corporations, Limited Partnerships, trusts, etc.) and their tax impacts.

- Consult with attorney to discuss legal implications of a partnership, the roles and responsibilities of each partner, and exposure to liability. Discuss other possible forms of business (corporations, Limited Partnerships, trusts, etc.) and their risk/ legal implications.

- Have an attorney draw up the final agreement.

Cash Advances from Credit Cards:

Another potential source of funding is cash advances from your credit cards. This can be a good source of financing. It is quick, easy, has no closing fees, and is very flexible. Monthly minimum payments are generally small, and the amount can be completely repaid without penalty at any time. If you are going to do this, just be careful not to get overextended so that you cannot make the monthly payment or have no reserve for an unexpected expense.

Friends and Family:

If you are like most people, you will find that many of your friends are nervous about what you are doing. They will tell you that buying real estate is a bad idea, and that you will lose money. I suggest that you do not talk to them about this until you find your first house. Once you find the house, invite them out to take a look at it. Take them through the house and tell them how much you can buy it for. Ask them if they would like to get involved. If you can buy a house that is worth $100,000 for $60,000, ask them if they would like to go into partnership with you by lending you the money to buy and fix-up the house in exchange for part of the profits. Once they see that you are actually able to buy a house worth $100,000 for $60,000, they might be a lot more interested and may want to participate.

It is even all right to put together a syndication of sorts where each syndicate member puts up some money in return for a share of the profits once the property is sold. Check with your attorney prior to accepting syndicated money because there are strict rules about syndication which require certain disclosures prior to your taking any money.

Self directed IRAs

Self directed IRAs can be another good source of financing. You can actually invest your own retirement money in real estate.

If you want to do a self directed IRA, you need to get competent professional tax and legal advice. Be sure to go to your accountant and possibly your lawyer (go to your accountant first) and find out what you need to do to set up the self directed IRA. There are companies that offer self-directed IRA administration that can help you as well. Check my internet directory for companies which manage self-directed IRAs.

Business Opportunities Advertising:

Look in the business opportunity section of the newspaper for people who lend money for new business "start ups." If you do not see any, place your own "Capital Wanted" ad. It might read: "$60,000 needed. Secured by residential real estate. 70% L.T.V.; 6 months payback; 13% interest." Be careful about anyone who approaches you about raising funds by putting together an LLC, limited partnership, corporation or other entity that people can buy into. There are strict rules about who you can accept money from without having to register the securities. For the most part you will only be able to accept money from "accredited investors" (meaning rich people) as that term is legally defined. If you are going to pursue money this way take one of my courses on raising private money. Check the website http://www. bobdiamondrealestate.com for a list of upcoming seminars or call our office at 800-608-0514.

If you are borrowing money, be careful of anyone who poses as a broker in this type of transaction. If you are going to deal with brokers, only deal with one who does not take an up front fee and only takes a percentage of the loan that he places. I have seen brokers try to extract thousands of dollars in fees at the time of application. Once they get the money from you, they tend to lose their motivation to work to get you a loan, and you are unlikely to get the loan that you expected.

Banks and Mortgage Companies

If you are employed, have good credit, and not too much debt, you should be able to borrow money for your deals. It is usually possible to get a loan which is 60% to 80% of the retail value of an investment property. It takes some time to line up this money, but lenders are usually comfortable in these situations because they are protected by the high value of the collateral, as compared to the amount of the loan, and will not lose any money if they have to foreclose. You cannot use this financing if you purchase at the foreclosure auction because there is not enough time between the auction and settling on the property. You can apply for institutional financing if you are buying a pre-foreclosure or R.E.O.

There are various bank and mortgage company loans which can finance your house purchase costs and your fix-up costs. You will have to contribute some percentage of your own money to the deal. This percentage will vary from one loan program to another, but as an investor you will generally need to put at least 15% to 30% of your own money into the project, and the bank will finance the rest. This percentage requirement applies regardless of whether or not you have bought the property at a discount. You will be eligible to borrow the lesser of 70% to 85% of the actual acquisition and fix up costs, or a 70% to 85% of the retail value of the property.

If you are purchasing as an owner/occupant, you can sometimes get as much as 97% financing, meaning you can finance 97% of the purchase price or the appraised value (whichever is lower), along with 97% of the fix up costs. You should ask your lender about the FHA 203K program, which is a loan program oriented towards the purchase and fix up of properties.

Small local banks, savings and loans, and credit unions who do a lot of business in the area where you are purchasing the house will often have flexible loan programs for use in purchasing local properties. You are looking for a small institution, which is what is called a "portfolio lender." A portfolio lender means that the institution is lending its own money and plans to keep the loan until it is paid off.

Larger institutions are a less likely place for you to get the money you need. Many lenders make loans intending to sell them. There are limitations in this way of conducting business. The biggest limitation from an investor's standpoint is that the lender must fit all of their loans into the requirements of the ultimate buyer of the loan. This means that the loan needs to conform to strict lending and administrative requirements. Because of this, these lenders cannot be flexible. If you find a local savings-and-loan, credit union, or other small bank or lending institution that does not sell their loans, you are more likely to get the flexibility that you need.

Financing with Cash:

Obviously this is the simplest method to pay for property. If you are going to finance your own properties with cash, you may want to use an indirect method. You might want to start a second entity, such as a corporation, limited partnership, limited liability corporation, or trust. These entities would have an impact on your tax situation and the liability associated with owning property.

Make an appointment with a competent real estate attorney and accountant to determine how to hold title to the properties to minimize your risks and maximize your tax advantages.

If you are just starting out and do not yet have a lot of money or assets, keep things simple and own properties in your own name. Although it might be ideal to designate an entity such as a corporation, trust, or limited partnership as owner of the property, most lenders will not lend money to such an entity and you can complicate your investing. To minimize your personal risk exposure when you are starting out, keep your properties insured, be sure contractors who work for you have liability and workers compensation insurance. Consult with an attorney and accountant when you have the money to do so.

Tax Alert!

An issue of which you should be aware if you are flipping properties is that the IRS can classify you as a "dealer." This means that you can never depreciate any rental property you may own. This can cause you to incur a substantial tax bill every year. To avoid this, if you plan on flipping properties, address the "dealer classification" issue with your accountant before you buy your first property. The issue can usually be addressed by separating the ownership of property you are holding for rental from those you are flipping. You may be advised to hold some property in a corporation, trust, or limited partnership, instead of in your own name. This way the separate entity can be the "dealer." This is an important issue and must be addressed before you flip your first property.

Section Seven

Final Thoughts
and Words

19

General Advice

Use a Cookie Cutter to Consistently find Deals and Make Profits

You have a better chance of making a profit in any business if you have one method of generating income that can be used over and over again. I refer to this as a "cookie cutter." Using a "cookie cutter" means that you should develop one system of consistently making profits and continue to apply that system over and over again. If you want to buy rental properties, focus on buying rentals and managing them. Do not simultaneously pursue properties to flip and properties to rent.

If you want to focus on properties to "flip," at first focus on doing one deal at a time. Do not get distracted by chasing more deals once you have one. Complete that deal and then move on to the next.

Wait Until You Find the Right Deal to Invest Your Money

After you have become familiar with the business, you will find that there are more potential deals than you have the time or money to invest in. Keep that in mind when you look at any particular deal. If the deal looks marginal, skip over that deal and start looking for another one. It is better to shop for a longer time and find a great deal than it is to buy the first thing you see and end up with a marginal deal.

Don't be Afraid to Make Low Offers

You can and should look for properties through multiple sources. As you become involved in real estate investing, real estate agents and others will tell you about properties. Listen to them and be aware that they MAY have a deal for you. Do not be afraid to ASK for what you WANT by making an offer based on what you are willing to pay, rather than on what someone is asking for the property. Do not be deterred by a real estate agent telling you "they will never accept that!" or "that offer would insult the seller!". If you want to go out with the prettiest girl, you need to ask her! The worst that will happen is the seller saying "no". If that happens, move on to the next property. You will occasionally be pleasantly surprised when a low offer is accepted by a seller. Sometimes they even call you months after the initial offer asking if you are still willing to buy! ASK FOR WHAT YOU REALLY WANT, OR YOU WILL NEVER GET WHAT YOU WANT!

Manage Your Own Properties

There is no one as interested in your real estate investment than you are. If you do not manage your real estate, it will almost inevitably not be managed profitably and you will find that you will have difficulty ever making money.

Stay Close to Home

If you ever make the mistake of investing in a long-term investment property which is more than an hour from your home, and you are forced to hire an agent to manage it and contractors to perform every tiny repair, you will soon learn that is not a profitable enterprise and you will regret ever buying the property. Keep that advice in mind if you are ever asked to buy a vacation property for the purpose of investment. It is fine to buy those properties because you like to vacation there or for short-term appreciation, but do not ever mistake it for a responsible long-term real estate investment when it is compared with a property which is within half an hour of your home.

Do Not Overlook Complex Deals

Do not avoid complexity. The more complicated the deal, the higher the potential profits and the less competition there is likely to be. Do not fear complexity as long as you have competent advice. Indicators of good deals which happen to be complicated include deals with large IRS liens on a property; properties encumbered by multiple mortgages where a senior lien which is small in relation to the value of the property is foreclosing; and properties which are vacant.

Beware of Property with Potential Environmental Problems

If a building was ever used as a gas station, auto repair shop, paint store, factory, or for any other purpose requiring the storage or use of toxic wastes or hazardous compounds, you should not buy that property at a foreclosure sale or in any sale where you cannot conduct environmental studies called "Phase I" prior to the purchase. The cost of cleaning up land can run into hundreds of thousands of dollars, especially if the water beneath the land has become contaminated. You may also find yourself subject to fines in addition to cleanup costs.

You need not have much involvement with the land to be fully liable for environmental cleanup costs. Merely being the successful bidder at a foreclosure sale may be enough to make you liable for the costs to clean up that property. You may be able to go back to a previous owner or tenant to recover the costs of cleaning up the prop-

> **Do not buy property with potential for environmental problems at the auction**
> Work out a deal either pre foreclosure or post foreclosure. At either of these stages, you will be able to do what is called your "due diligence" work (which will include the environmental studies) before you commit to purchasing the property. Be sure to use an experienced real estate attorney if you are purchasing property with any environmental issues.

erty, but to do so would involve litigation, which will involve expending money for attorneys and a long waiting period between the time that you sued and the time you might collect any money from another party. The previous landowner or user may also not have any money to pay you, which means that you can get stuck with the bill. In short, avoid the problem in

the first place by screening the property for environmental problems before becoming involved with a commercial property.

How to Measure the Risk of Environmental Problems There are generally two kinds of studies done to determine the likelihood of any environmental problems. The first kind of study is called a "Phase I" study. In a Phase I study, an environmental engineering firm sends someone to visit the site to look for evidence or indications of environmental problems. They also check public records for any indication of spills at the site, nearby toxic waste sites, and previous uses of the property involving hazardous waste. The environmental firm also checks for the presence of any underground storage tanks, which may have caused contamination.

After the Phase I study is completed, if the engineering firm suspects possible environmental problems, a "Phase II" study will be recommended. A Phase II study involves taking soil samples from the land and analyzing them to detect any hazardous compounds. It might also involve testing any underground storage tanks for leakage. In Philadelphia, a typical cost to check a small property for Phase I problems would between $1,300 to $1,500. The Phase II study is more expensive and depends upon what was found during Phase I.

20

Conclusion

Thank you for taking the time to read this book. I hope it has been educational and enjoyable. I want to wish you good luck in applying the information and reaching your goals.

If you read this book carefully, follow my advice and, most importantly, LOOK AT POTENTIAL DEALS AND HOUSES EVERY MONTH, then make offers once you identify a deal. The material in this book can only work if you take action!

If people are not successful investors, it is usually for one of two reasons. The most common reason is they do not spend enough time looking for deals. The terminology in this business can be confusing but the basic business is simple - buy property at a discount and either rent it out or sell it for a profit. Do not be afraid that you do not know enough to look at potential deals.

Once you find a willing seller or a vacant house with equity, the technical details of closing or evaluating the deal can be accomplished with the help of experts such as an attorney, real estate agent, or contractor. Even if you are just a beginner you can use my methods to locate and identify the deal and then draw upon professional help to sort out the details. Learn what you can from my book and then spend your time looking at the houses in foreclosure. Refer back to my books and retain professionals to help you once you find a potential deal.

The second reason people do not purchase is they do not actually make the purchase once they identify the deal. You may be spending a large sum of money to make the purchase and it is normal to have some fear of spending. There are two good solutions to this problem. The first is to hire knowledgeable professionals and trust them to help you. A good real estate attorney is the best professional to help you avoid the legal pitfalls of a foreclosure. A real estate agent or appraiser is the best one to help you set the proper value on a property. Do not try to get these people to work for free. They will not do a thorough job for you if you are trying to "pick their brain". Formally hire them and they will do their job right. A second solution to the problem of not moving forward is to team up with an experienced and successful investor to do the deal together. The toughest part of the foreclosure game is finding the deal. Once you find the deal you are in a position to pick a partner and negotiate a good compensation package for yourself. A typical deal would be either a ten percent finders fee (10% of the cost to purchase the property) or a 50-50 profit split. Typically the experienced investor will line up the money and direct the project and the less experienced investor will do a lot of the foot-work and on-site work. You can learn a lot from an experienced investor and when the experienced investors profit is on the line they will pay attention to the details and teach you how to do a deal profitably. Be careful in choosing your partner. Check into a potential partners reputation before letting them in on your deal. If they have a reputation of dishonesty, incompetence, or no track record of success in the type of venture you are doing, do not partner with them. A good place to find a partner is at your local real estate investor club. If you do not know where a local club is in your area call NAREIA at 888-

7NAREIA (888-762-7342). If you are on the internet, you can look up a list of groups at the NAREIA web-site "HTTP://WWW.NAREIA.COM."

Be nosy. Be diligent. Be persistent. You can and will succeed!

THE END

This is the end of this book but hopefully the beginning of your investing career!

Please write me at bob@bobdiamond.com to let me know how you are doing. I especially love to hear testimonials and also about any errors in the book or forms that you need that are not in the forms set.

Also, check our website http://www.bobdiamondrealestate.com or call our office at 800-608-0514 if you need information about our other products and services.